Body and Soul

THE LIBRARY OF OBJECT RELATIONS

A Series of Books Edited By
David E. Scharff and Jill Savege Scharff

Object relations theories of human interaction and development provide an expanding, increasingly useful body of theory for the understanding of individual development and pathology, for generating theories of human interaction, and for offering new avenues of treatment. They apply across the realms of human experience from the internal world of the individual to the human community, and from the clinical situation to everyday life. They inform clinical technique in every format from individual psychoanalysis and psychotherapy, through group therapy, to couple and family therapy.

The Library of Object Relations aims to introduce works that approach psychodynamic theory and therapy from an object relations point of view. It includes works from established and new writers who employ diverse aspects of British, American, and international object relations theory in helping individuals, families, couples, and groups. It features books that stress integration of psychoanalytic approaches with marital, family, and group therapy, as well as those centered on individual psychotherapy and psychoanalysis.

Refinding the Object and Reclaiming the Self
David E. Scharff

The Primer of Object Relations Therapy
Jill Savege Scharff and David E. Scharff

Object Relations Couple Therapy
David E. Scharff and Jill Savege Scharff

From Inner Sources:
New Directions in Object Relations Psychotherapy
N. Gregory Hamilton, Ed.

Object Relations Family Therapy
David E. Scharff and Jill Savege Scharff

Projective and Introjective Identification and the Use of the Therapist's Self
Jill Savege Scharff

Foundations of Object Relations Family Therapy
Jill Savege Scharff, Ed.

The Practice of Psychoanalytic Therapy
Karl König

Repairing Intimacy:
An Object Relations Approach to Couples Therapy
Judith Siegel

Family and Couple Therapy
John Zinner

Close Encounters:
A Relational View of the Therapeutic Process
Robert Winer

The Autonomous Self:
The Work of John D. Sutherland
Jill Savege Scharff, Ed.

Crisis at Adolescence:
Object Relations Therapy with the Family
Sally Box et al., Eds.

Personal Relations Therapy: The Collected Papers of H. J. S. Guntrip
Jeremy Hazell, Ed.

Psychoanalytic Group Psychotherapy
Karl König and Wulf-Volker Lindner

Countertransference Analysis
Karl König

Object Relations Theory and Practice
David E. Scharff, Ed.

On Freud's Couch:
Seven New Interpretations of Freud's Case Histories
Iréne Matthis and Imre Szecsödy, Eds.

From Instinct to Self:
Selected Papers of W.R.D. Fairbairn, Volume I: Clinical and Theoretical Contributions
David E. Scharff and Ellinor Fairbairn Birtles, Eds.

From Instinct to Self:
Selected Papers of W.R.D. Fairbairn, Volume II: Applications and Early Contributions
Ellinor Fairbairn Birtles and David E. Scharff, Eds.

Object Relations Therapy of Physical and Sexual Trauma
Jill Savege Scharff and David E. Scharff

Object Relations Individual Therapy
Jill Savege Scharff and David E. Scharff

A Prophetic Analyst:
Erich Fromm's Contributions to Psychoanalysis
Mauricio Cortina and Michael Maccoby, Eds.

Intricate Engagements:
The Collaborative Basis of Therapeutic Change
Steven A. Frankel

A Primer of Kleinian Therapy
Irving Solomon

Containing Rage, Terror, and Despair:
An Object Relations Approach to Psychotherapy
Jeffrey Seinfeld

Object Relations Brief Therapy
Michael Stadter

Love and Hate in the Analytic Setting
Glen O. Gabbard

Cruelty, Violence, and Murder:
Understanding the Criminal Mind
Arthur Hyatt-Williams

Body and Soul:
The Role of Object Relations in Faith, Shame, and Healing
Harold E. Bronheim

How to Survive as a Psychotherapist
Nina Coltart

The Sexual Relationship:
An Object Relations View of Sex and the Family
David E. Scharff

Body and Soul

The Role of Object Relations in Faith, Shame, and Healing

Harold E. Bronheim, M.D.

JASON ARONSON INC.
Northvale, New Jersey
London

This book was set in 11 pt. Century Schoolbook and printed and bound by Book-mart Press of North Bergen, New Jersey.

Library of Congress Cataloging-in-Publication Data

Bronheim, Harold.
    Body and soul : the role of object relations in faith, shame, and healing / by Harold Bronheim.
        p. cm.
    ISBN 0-7657-0162-6
    1. Object relations (Psychoanalysis) 2. Shame. 3. Faith.
    4. Faith. I. Title.
    RC455.4.O23B76 1998
    616.89'17—dc21   98-10729

Printed in the United States of America on acid-free paper. For information and catalog write to Jason Aronson Inc., 230 Livingston Street, Northvale, New Jersey 07647-1726. Or visit our website: http://www.aronson.com

To my mother, Rose
who taught me courage.

To my father, Sol
who taught me humility.

To my wife, Annette
who taught me grace.

To my daughters, Elisabeth and Julia
who taught me joy.

Contents

Preface

This has been the century of psychoanalysis in modern psychiatry. Some in the analytic community, however, are beginning to feel that psychoanalysis is a mature field that has peaked, with little fundamentally new to say. By comparison, brain science in the last decade has regularly produced new discoveries that revise or remold older theories of brain physiology and function. So often now, the psychoanalytic literature seems to have devolved into circular discussions of well-established principles or extensive reviews of previous work updated to modern practice. Is analysis busy just writing its own history, but otherwise has reached the natural limit of its own domain? Is there really anything new to say?

Body and Soul is an unusual title for a psychoanalytic text, one that strives to be both rational and clinically reasonable. Object relations theory is a well-regarded theoretical framework upon which one can build an understanding of the dynamic interactions in the therapeutic setting. What could it possibly have to do with "soul"? This book also raises the question: What are the implications of object relations theory for the perception of "truth"? Can a book that touches upon this issue be taken seriously, let alone be considered truthful?

These are some of the questions I would have, if asked to consider the worthiness of the arguments made in the following chapters. On the other hand, in a mature field like psy-

choanalysis, one does not often have the opportunity to ex-
plore subjects that have not already been seriously considered by many writers and practitioners in the past. In many
cases we are largely repackaging old concepts in new contain-
ers, and by so doing hopefully re-creating something fresh and
alive. In the chapters ahead we will try instead to take analysis through object relations theory into new domains that
have been avoided in the past mainly because they were considered not applicable—for example, religion and faith because of Freud's clear opposition to them, and the body because of a preoccupation of late with mind in the mind–body
split.

This book could bring the reader to unanticipated and possibly undesirable conclusions that may be irritating or hard
to accept. The intent here, however, is not to convince read-
ers of some absolute belief in one truth or another, but rather
to intrigue them with the possibility of the theoretical and
clinical application of incorporating a broader perspective. Although my analyst's analyst's analyst was analyzed by Freud,
and they have all transmitted a classical ego psychology orientation down to me, I, by temperament and circumstance,
have been forced to practice within a wider scope because of
the patient population it has been my good fortune to treat.

There are many thanks to be offered in preparation of such
a work. First, my teachers Drs. Edmund Slakter, James
Strain, and Edward Joseph—all of whom are or were members of the New York Psychoanalytic Institute—need to be
singled out, not only as great supervisors and teachers but also
as humanitarians. A special thanks also to Dr. Stephen
Snyder, who has spent many hours with me in peer supervision. I would also like to thank Dr. Jill Savege Scharff, who
invited me to produce this work and who encouraged me in
the effort.

Introduction

Turn, turn, my wheel! This earthen jar
A touch can make, a touch can mar;
And shall it to the potter say,
What makest thou? Thou hast no hand?
As men who think to understand
A world by their creator planned
Who wiser is than they.
                —Henry Wadsworth Longfellow, "Keramos"

Patients come to therapy because they suffer. The signs and symptoms of their suffering are categorized into disorders to enable us to better understand the nature of their problems and the means with which to help them. Although the patient may not be continuously conscious of it, from the first session to the last there is fear and pain; even if it is not apparent, it is always there.

It is the suffering of our patients that is at the root of the constant struggle to improve our working theory and strengthen our clinical deliberations. Psychoanalysis strives to be universally applicable, not for its own sake, but because suffering is the one promise that life always keeps. Additions to psychoanalytic theory or practice are accepted if they add to the alleviation of suffering; otherwise they are of no benefit. Too often we lose sight of this fundamental concern and become, instead, ideological proponents of one theory or another. In doing so we become brainless or mindless, depending on our particular orientation; either way, the result is heartless.

Many psychiatrists believe that patients who present with symptoms that meet even the minimal criteria for a mental disorder should be treated with medication as the primary approach. In many instances that is exactly correct, as, for example, in clear-cut cases of intractable obsessive-compulsive disorder or acute mania. It is not the case, however, for many others who come to us seeking help. The benefits of medication have been demonstrated almost exclusively in studies where patients with severe character disorders or complicating medical illnesses have been conveniently excluded. Therefore, the basis for the use and the indications for medication in many patients with these co-morbid conditions is far from clear.

This is not to say that abnormal biological states and traits do not coexist with mental disorders or do not contribute significantly to individual suffering. In fact, mental symptoms that may result entirely from psychological causes—as for example in grief resulting from loss—may, with chronicity, bring about physiological changes that are manifest in depression. Furthermore, from the outset children have their own unique temperaments and affective coloring that influence their experience of the world about them. They are not merely passive social beings; they insist on practicing their own unique skills and habits that have been acquired through effort. By virtue of both temperament and personal behavior, children are susceptible to dysregulation and personal suffering.

However, it is also certainly true that developing children cannot survive long without nurturing parents. To think of development or psychopathology as merely biologically self-arising or self-contained is absurd. The nature and quality of the relationship with the primary caregiver is clearly the most important variable in the development of character. It is for this reason that object-relations theory is rapidly be-

coming the most universally accepted paradigm in psychoanalysis.

In any event, the way that mental distress is dealt with
by individuals the world around generally has very little to
do with psychiatry or psychoanalysis. In the first place, depression, anxiety, and other mental symptoms are expressed
primarily in the somatic form (Stoudemire 1991); and secondly, the understanding of their temporal occurrence is
linked to general explanations associated with experiences
arising from the social context, or to derivations of meaning
from the religious realm.

Psychoanalysis has not made a deep impression with a significant portion of the world's societies because it does not
readily incorporate attitudes with regard to body image and
disease on one hand and feelings with regard to religion and
faith on the other. By essentially holding itself apart from
these areas (so as not to be corrupted by their nonscientific
beliefs), psychoanalysis has probably slowed its own introduction. Simple psychoanalytic explanations of religious beliefs
and attitudes have failed to capture the inherent essence of
their ideational power—*faith*. Similarly, early, simplistic
cause-and-effect psychosomatic explanations of disease causation failed to deal with the far greater psychological com-
plexity that surrounds illness behavior.

In this book we will take a broad new look at these issues.
The first chapter is a brief, general overview of object relations theory. Object relations, as we will show, is a very big
tent capable of enclosing participants of many different ori-
entations. The historical roots of object relations in the British School are reviewed, and compared to the classical ego
psychology model. Stated simply, in the classical ego psychology model the core drives seek gratification and pleasure, the
defense of whose expression leads to anxiety and symptom
formation. In object relations theory, the drives seek attachment to an object. The ramifications of this change in orientation for analytic understanding and analytic stance are
substantial and are elaborated upon. There is also a discus-

sion of the work of Kernberg and Kohut, both of whom have been critically influential in the analytic field by opening the path from the unitary classical system to the multi-variegated object relations system. Although not fully agreed upon or accepted in all quarters of the psychoanalytic community, object relations theory is rapidly becoming the epistemological basis for modern psychoanalysis.

In Chapter 2 the implications of object relations for understanding faith are examined. Instead of viewing faith as a curious concept of a singularly religious nature, we attempt to demonstrate that it is an absolutely essential core issue in psychological development in its relation to object constancy. There are countless religious individuals who have very little real faith in an open sense, and many other irreligious and atheistic individuals of deep and abiding faith. It is often the religious who, without real faith, are quick to condemn and judge others and the first to aggress against their neighbors—and sanctimoniously.

For the most part, psychoanalysis has been silent about faith and religion within the dyadic analytic relationship. However, insofar as faith is a core and central organizing state, its vicissitudes may be observed throughout the analysis if only one thinks to look for them. Faith develops as a product of analysis as a result of the relationship with the analyst, and cure can be measured by the nature and depth of the faith that is ultimately held by the analysand. This applies to all patients, religious or otherwise, and is not especially related to belief in God. Although the content of each person's beliefs may vary, those beliefs are far less important than the nature of the underlying faith.

Chapter 3 discusses the relationship of object relations to body image. Although, Freud, as a neurologist, strongly believed that his mental theory was somehow directly connected to the body, in successive reworkings of psychoanalytic theory by him and by many others the mind has become split off from the body. Yet, as mentioned above, most mental suffering is expressed in the somatic realm, and *all* physical suffering has mental as well as interpersonal components.

In this section we elaborate on the work of others to show how, in the infant, the mental self and the external object are not much differentiated from the body. Physical tension is relieved by physical contact with the primary object, and affects associated with the relationship between self and object are experienced directly in the body. Later in life, loss of important objects or parts of valued objects is experienced not only in the psychological realm of the self but also in the physical realm of the body. Conversely, injury to the body, or illness, leads to clinging interpersonal behavior and the search for securing if not omnipotent objects. Body image is not merely one's superficial physical appearance but, in fact, an amalgam of all aspects of the self—mental or physical, internal and external.

There are clear clinical benefits of developing a wider understanding of faith and body image. We can more completely relate to and discuss with our patients their essential concerns while simultaneously enlarging the immediate analytic exploration. We can explain more varied symptoms and relate more fully to existential, interpersonal, or physical issues. But, in addition, we are capable of more fully developing an understanding of a special affective symptom that is often neglected but is nevertheless deeply and painfully rooted in the psyche—*shame.*

Shame is a natural crosswalk between body and soul. One may suffer shame with regard to one's body or one may suffer shame with regard to one's soul. Usually, patients suffer both. In Chapter 4 we review the subject of shame, which, despite its ubiquity, in the psychoanalytic literature is poorly differentiated from guilt, from which it is clearly different— and yet it is the cause of so much suffering. Shame is clearly related to object relations because, by necessity, it requires an observer and an observed. Shame is not merely learned, it is inculcated—often at a very early age. It involves humiliation, aggression, and threats of isolation, and when done to excess results in severe character disorder. In this manner, it is connected to both poor body image and deficits in faith, conditions that generally occur in individuals who are acutely disturbed by shame.

Analytic theory usually follows clinical practice. Our discussion of the role of object relations in faith, body image, and shame has been derived from working with patients with complex co-morbid illnesses who have not responded to previous treatments, or for whom standard treatment (analysis) would not ordinarily be recommended. In Chapter 5 we discuss the implications of some of the above considerations for alterations in technique, especially with regard to the analytic stance. With persons who suffer from severe character disturbance a more active stance is essential, one whose vectors are oriented to draw in the analysand as closely as they can tolerate, in object relations terms, before the eruption of overwhelming panic and aggression. Although this is difficult to maintain, it is necessary in order to create a new working alliance that can withstand the intensity of the resultant projective identifications. An extended discussion of this view is presented in the treatment of one such individual, Ms. A., whose course in psychoanalytic psychotherapy was sustained by application of these variations in technique.

Naturally, when one discusses faith, religion, and other psychological issues, one cannot help but consider the issue of truth. Many questions immediately arise with regard to the question of truth, not only with regard to the issues we have been discussing so far, but also with regard to larger questions such as: "Is object relations, as a theory, true?" Further issues that must be examined include questions such as: "Are reminiscences derived in analysis true?" and "Is analysis true even though it may not be rigorously verifiable and therefore not scientific in the classic tradition?" We address some of these issues in Chapter 6 by examining the implications for truth itself, assuming its psychological derivation from object relations. Object relations always result in a dichotomy that makes singular truths impossible. The search for the one unitary truth and the making of grand synthetic theories, whether in science, religion, or psychiatry (brain and psyche), we believe, reflects our unforgotten, unavowed, and unrelinquished wish for fusion with the lost idealized objects of early childhood. We may wish for such perfect truth, but it is ephemeral and not to be found except on brief occasions.

1

Object Relations

Oedipus: "What miseries could ever let you leave unsolved the death and downfall of a king? . . . I'll go back and drag that shadowed past to light again."
—Sophocles, *Oedipus the King*

In the broadest terms, psychoanalytic object relations theory represents the psychoanalytic study of the nature of interpersonal relations and their development within the mental structure of the mind and the self through the internalization of early parent–child interactions. Object relations theory is commonly assumed to imply the theory and practice of psychoanalysis as it was formulated by the "British School"— including Ronald Fairbairn, Donald Winnicott, Harry Guntrip, Michael Balint, and to a lesser extent Melanie Klein. Although it most certainly includes the aforementioned practitioners, object relations theory has been more widely incorporated into psychoanalytic theory and practice and includes the work of many others noteworthy among whom are Kernberg (1984), Erikson (1956), Jacobson (1964), Mahler (1967), Kohut (1978), and J. Scharff (1992). Although the development of object relations theory also includes the work of Sullivan and Horney, object relations can in fact be traced back to Freud, especially in regard to his early delineation of transference. However, to appreciate the full meaning and contribution of object relations theory to modern psychoanalysis, it is important to understand its deviation from classical psychoanalysis.

DRIVE THEORY

The classical drive/ego psychology model is a structural theory of the mind that views the mind as a socially interactive, but otherwise self-contained functional unit. In arranging it so, Freud adhered to the scientific method, in which he discussed the mechanisms of a separately observed, independently functional, biologically driven entity. In its most essential nature, classical analytic theory (or the "structural model") begins with libidinous drives or instincts that seek satisfaction, gratification, and pleasure, while simultaneously avoiding wherever possible frustration or pain. On the other hand, as society and the world at large respond to the dependent child, either to satisfy or frustrate its drives, the child is led to a differentiation of mental structure (Freud 1915a,b). On the basis of his early work with patients, Freud first separated the structure of mind into the unconscious and conscious. The unconscious involved primary process, biologically determined, impulse-ridden thinking; the conscious was dominated by reality-based secondary process, reasoning, and rationality. In this model of the mind "the organism seeks: the discharge of instinctual tension; repetition of tension-reducing behavior so as to return to a state of homeostasis; or narcissistic retreat into the self, where needs either do not disturb or their satisfaction can be imagined as vividly as if they were occurring" (Scharff and Scharff 1995, p 13) Elements of unprocessed drives can erupt into consciousness in dreams, slips of the tongue, and psychological symptoms, and, through a psychoanalytic process of "free association," Freud discovered that these unconscious wishes could be brought under control of consciousness, leading to the relief of symptoms.

Freud reorganized his theory later into the tripartite structural model of the id, ego, and superego (Freud 1923). In this model, the id is the wellspring of the biological drives of life, including thirst, hunger, sexuality, aggression, and so on, which seek immediate satisfaction. The ego is the master planner and organizer that facilitates the expression of the drives in a fashion that is situationally appropriate and adaptive to the world at large. The ego mediates the expression of the internal drives within the constraints of outer reality. The superego, on the other hand, is a set of internal identifications that serve to limit the full expression of the drives, depending on whether or not they are appropriate to the circumstances. As such, it is the internal modulator of restricted moral behavior and the center for the development of the qualities of the ego ideals.

Anxiety, which is ubiquitous in psychiatric conditions, was thought by Freud to be a signal of the inappropriate and potentially dangerous expression of the drives. Defenses employed by the ego divert the full, uncensored expression of the drives and therefore shape the features of "neurotic" symptoms (e.g., compulsions, phobias, and so on), or organize the general structure of an individual's character.

Classical analytic theory has been expanded and elaborated upon by many practitioners since Freud. Anna Freud (1946) delineated a wide range of defenses. Heinz Hartmann (1964) discussed the adaptive nature of the ego, leading to "ego psychology." Wilhelm Reich (1949) introduced character types, while Fenichel (1945) and Glover (1949) applied the structural model to a wider range of psychiatric conditions. Brenner (1982) brought attention to the centrality of conflict, and Gill (1982), Arlow (1989), Greenson (1971), and others focused on the importance of transference, countertransference, and the real relationship with the analysand. Because of their modifications and the contributions of many others, the theory of the drive structural model has evolved—so much so that nowadays it is generally recognized that the ego defenses employed for the adaptive expression of the drives and protection of the child's vulnerabilities are made for the fulfillment of its needs, especially with regard to primary relationships. Thus "defenses such as projection, denial, displacement, sublimation, reversal of affect and reaction formation can all be seen as ways of structuring relationships" (Scharff and Scharff 1995, p. 19).

In the classical model, mental structure—both adaptive and pathological—is built from the ground up, and it differentiates along the way to the psychic whole of the proactive independent self. This model was the dominant analytic paradigm for five decades, especially in the United States until the early 1980s. Classical ego psychology thrived in the United States because of the powerful emphasis on the uniqueness and responsibility of the individual enshrined in the social concept of "freedom," and because of society's strong attachment to the scientific method, with its reliance on the impartial and detached observer. The notion of a being as first and foremost self-existing, self-developing, and self-acting—pursuing the satisfaction of its own desires—was considered reasonable if not self-evident. Internal development of the psychic structure of the child in response to the demands of a more powerful outer reality of adults fit neatly with the societal view of America as a "melting pot" where each individual is first and foremost free to pursue his or her own happiness—but within the limits of socially controlled boundaries.

SELF PSYCHOLOGY

In the 1970s, Heinz Kohut, an influential member of the classical school of analysis, developed a relational-based, self psychological analytic theory, as a result of disappointing experiences in treating narcissistic personalities with the classical approach. Whereas in the standard theory it was believed that the deepest level of the mind had been reached when the patient experienced the immediate full force of the uncensored wishes and drives that constitute the neurotic conflict, Kohut theorized that the neurotic conflict was itself embedded in a deeper self-selfobject disturbance. Beneath the conflict of forbidden impulses lay a deeper layer of narcissistic rage and depression as a result of empathic failures (Kohut 1984, p. 5).

For Kohut (1977) the self is "a center of initiative and re-cipient of impressions" (p. 99). The self is more than a de-rivative representation of the ego and is itself an active agent and source of motivation. The self maintains internal homeo-stasis through a closeness maintained with empathic selfobjects. Failures of empathy on the part the selfobject lead to narcissistic defects and anxiety about self dissolution. Moreover, the need for mirroring selfobjects is continuous and necessary throughout the life cycle. Although the self built from early self-selfobject relations is a permanent part of the mental structure it nevertheless may be significantly modi-fied by later relationships, especially when they are empathic.

For Kohut, the self psychological model was complemen-tary to the classical model. Although symptoms may be in part the manifestation of neurotic conflict, the neurotic con-flict itself arises as a result of a struggle at a deeper level for a cohesive and integrated self and occurs at every age when the individual is threatened by loss of the primary object. Anxiety arises not just as a result of a regression from the oedipal conflict and the threatened eruption of forbidden im-pulses, but from the whole self under pressure, threatening to break into parts. In the self-psychological model, the child at every stage of development comes to relationships already a whole entity, seeking empathy to maintain cohesion. This is in marked contrast to the structural model, in which pri-mary libidinous and aggressive drives must first be molded and organized by successively higher ego defenses before they finally evolve into the mental structure of a representative self.

DEVELOPMENTAL THEORY

Concurrent with these analytic movements, developmental child psychiatrists, as a result of their direct observation and study of children, were now for the first time able to provide more definitive data on the early history of object relations. They observed that the self, as something distinct from the object, arose as a direct outcome of multiple mother–child interactions. At approximately 15 to 18 months of age, in Mahler's so-called rapprochement phase, the child becomes aware that the mother is not only a source of security but actually a separate entity (Mahler et al. 1975, pp. 90–95). Basic trust formed in the first year in the underlying relationship by the individuating child and the consistency of the parental object gives way to object constancy and the development of faith in the parental object, faith in the object's reappearance, and, through association, the beginnings of object constancy, as reflected by the child's faith in itself. At this stage of development (in the middle of the second to the third year of life) the child's development centers around autonomy versus shame and doubt, as its interest and attention shift from self interest and exploration to social interaction (Parens 1989).

OBJECT RELATIONS

The term "object" was first used by Freud (1915b) with regard to the vicissitudes of the drives and how they find expression by attachment to objects. He chose the term *object* because in his clinical work with patients with psychopathology it was clear that they had libidinous attachments which were displaced, not necessarily always onto other human beings. Some objects are decidedly inanimate, such as drugs are for an addicted person, or a hard surface for an autistic child. Some objects are referred to as *transitional* and include a favored stuffed animal or blanket. In object-relations theory, the object is decidedly human although it may be more or less depersonified (e.g., an attachment to a part of the person [breast] or to a primitive experience of the person).

Fairbairn (1941) originated the fundamental premise of object relations: that libido and the remainder of drive derivatives are object-seeking. In a preface to Fairbairn (1952), Ernest Jones (Freud's biographer) wrote: "If it were possible to condense Dr. Fairbairn's new ideas into one sentence it might run somewhat as follows. Instead of starting as Freud did from stimulation of the nervous system proceeding from excitation of various erogenous zones and internal tension arising from gonadic activity, Dr. Fairbairn starts at the center of the personality, the ego, and depicts its strivings and difficulties in its endeavour to reach an object where it may find support" (Jones 1952, p. v).

Object-relations theory begins from within a different frame of reference. Instead of drives seeking satisfaction and the minimum of displeasure, drives seek attachment and love. In this frame of reference it is thought simplistic to consider a human individual developing as a self-contained unit. A human grows in utero fused within the body of the mother and then postpartum remains intimately attached for many years thereafter. The infant is completely dependent upon the mother and it develops as a result of the attachment to her and the multiple experiences with separation. In Fairbairn's (1952) view, ego development is characterized by a process whereby an original state of infantile dependence based upon primary identification with the object is abandoned in favor of a state of mature dependence based upon differentiation of the object from the self. Even an ideal maternal object through absence or failure to gratify the infant instantaneously will be experienced as frustrating or rejecting, or conversely, as overstimulating and exciting, leading to the formation of internal object relations and differentiation of the self. It is these multiple experiences with the mother that are internalized into the building blocks of mental structure. However, the experience is seldom neutral; the relationship internalized is affectively colored and may be either gratifying or painful.

Even though many years later such practitioners from the classical school as Brenner (1982) would lift the "drives" out of the biology of the body and retain them only as a metaphor, Fairbairn's reworking of the nature of the drives was in his time considered radical and divorced from the first causes of biology. It awaited the arrival of Bowlby (1960), an ethnologist and infant researcher, to state that all social mammals are physiologically preprogrammed to attachment as an evolutionary protective mechanism the interruption of which is associated with separation anxiety and disturbances in affect.

The mechanism by which internal object relations are formed, as described by Fairbairn, is as theoretical as Freud's system. According to J. Scharff (1992), object relations are formed through projective identifications. The infant projects onto the parent its needs and desires, and identifies its needs in the mother. The mother comforts the infant by correct recognition of its needs. The manner in which the parent identifies and responds to the infant is internalized by the child. If the child's needs are ignored or rejected, the rejection is internalized and the child experiences itself as hostile. If the parent responds with excessive overanxious concern, that is also internalized, and the child experiences itself as excited and craving.

A more comprehensive delineation of object relations theory was made by Kernberg (1984). In his view, object relations transcended any particular psychoanalytic school and represented a general psychoanalytic development that included practitioners from the classical ego psychology school, Schafer (1968) and Modell (1968); members of the British School, Winnicott (1955), Guntrip (1971), and Sutherland (1963); as well as others, such as Jacobson (1964) and Mahler and colleagues (1975).

According to Kernberg,

> Unconscious intrapsychic conflicts are never simply conflicts between impulse and defense; rather, the drive derivative finds expression through a certain primitive object relation (a certain unit of self-and-object representation); and the defense too is reflected by a certain internalized object relation. The conflict is between these intrapsychic structures. [Kernberg 1980, p. 155]

The child develops as a result of an integrated set of internalizations of self and object memories and experiences, together with their associated affects, forming object relation units (Kernberg 1984, pp. 56–58). Early in life, when the infant is fused with the mother or father, these units of object relations are highly amorphous and incomplete. A memory of a face, depersonified and detached from the rest of the body, may be introjected with an affect that is pleasant and positive or at other times unpleasant and negative. These amorphous disjointed experiences are separated, or "split" on the basis of pleasant or aversive affect. As the mind and brain develop, the introjects organize to form more cohesive and differentiated representations of the self and objects. When they have reached a certain level of organization in substance and memory where they are no longer split or separated by simple positive or negative affects, all subsequent interactions are referred to as being internalized. The stable integration of the split object relationship is an important milestone in mental development. Identification, a later developmental process, involves a self even more differentiated from the object, with the integration within the child of a copy of the behavior of the parent—either in thought or action, or in their role function at work, play, or social interaction.

The good and bad introjects are initially maintained separately both because they are markedly divergent in affect quality, but later also because of the anxiety associated with the possibility of premature merger. Some individuals suffering from what are usually referred to as borderline states (Knight 1953) fail to resolve the split between good and bad representations of the object. They usually do maintain conscious awareness of their divergent feelings with regard to the object, but with little insight into the consequences of the abrupt transition in relating to the good or bad representation of the object. Although it is not known why splitting is not resolved developmentally, it may be due to the effects of trauma associated with dissociation and chronic posttraumatic anxiety in physiologically reactive individuals. Dissociative events are frequently observed in borderline characters, as is a history of sexual or physical abuse. The younger a child is and the more frequently it suffers trauma and abuse, the more susceptible it is to dissociative events.

Less pathological and more cohesively organized object representations may still have profoundly unpleasant affects and aggression associated with their internal representations. In the service of the homeostatic functioning of the self, the negative or hateful representation of the internal object relation is repressed out of consciousness rather than being maintained in a split state. The more negative the affects associated with the internal object that must be repressed, whether sexually excitatory or aggressively hated, the more immature and unstable the ego remains, and the more punitive and rigid a superego is developed. Thus the individual remains with primitive characterological defenses to defend against the anxiety associated with the emergence of the more primitive self–object relation, while the superego berates the self with chronic shame and a sense of failure.

It is these repressed parts of the internal object relation, either excitatory and associated with craving, or painful and associated with aggression, or both, that are projected onto the analyst in treatment. Freud first referred to this process as *transference*, the examination and understanding of which represented the first analytic approach to object relations.

The developing child is not merely a passive actor in its own developmental history. All along the way, it projects the repressed parts of its internal object relations, as well as the unrepressed parts, onto the parental figure, and the responses are also internalized, as refinements of the original self–object relationship. This active projective identification leads to an ongoing reprocessing of the internal object relationship so that the parental figure is continuously being used as a mirror. Failure on the part of the parental figure to adequately metabolize the negative projections as well as empathic failures in new interactions leads to internalizations that make the child feel devalued, and the anxiety from this is defended against through the creation of a more grandiose narcissistic self.

MODERN PSYCHOANALYSIS

Mental structure, therefore, is built of multiple internal object relations, including parts that are repressed, and all
human beings have them. Our internal object relations interact continuously with those of the individuals around us
in a reciprocal and mutual fashion. The more intimately involved we become with others in relationships the more likely
it is that the repressed parts of the internal object relations
will become manifest, together with their powerful or painful affects. Two other conditions that lead to the emergence
of repressed internal object relations include (1) physiological derangement, for example physical disease, pain, drugs,
and so on, and (2) experiences of loss. Physical illness and
the loss of important objects and the affects associated with
grief are especially important in the shaping, or reactivating,
of feelings surrounding internal object relations.

Object-relations theory has had a profound effect upon psychoanalytic technique insofar as it has justified a shift from
a narrowly limited position of the therapist as a "blank
screen" of neutral observation and interpretation to a wider
range of modes of interaction adjusted by empathic participation. Although the more neutral observing stance is still
most appropriate for more advanced personality structures
with moderately neurotic symptoms, a more active and seemingly natural stance is appropriate in most other relationships. In fact analysts cannot help but introduce their own
spontaneous subjectivity into the process; they are practically
sucked into the patient's world, and it is the recognition of
these *countertransference reactions* that has enabled a convergence in psychoanalytic theorizing in the past decade
(Gabbard 1995).

As a result, modern psychoanalysis, informed by
object-relations theory, is more flexible and helpful for patients with a wider range of psychopathology, as well as for
those who may not be as given to introspection and free association. Concurrently, the nature of the content of analysis

has shifted from a primary focus on recovering in exact detail the history and memory of the analysand to the dynamic of the dyadic relationship that is being experienced in the here and now as it is distorted by the projected elements of long-repressed internal object relations. Psychoanalytic psychotherapy (in the post-ego psychology era) involves an exploration of unconscious internal objects as they are projected onto the therapist within the transference, and an analysis of the ways in which the patient resists those efforts to alter their perceptions despite the actual experience with the new therapist object (Ogden 1984).

Freud's first important discovery was the unconscious, and what he found there was an amazing wellspring of forbidden impulses and wishes. His delineation of instinctual biological drives was a natural outcome of his training as a neurologist. His clinical observations and his theoretical speculation joined to form a theory of symptoms and behavior that allowed for an innovative treatment of a wide range of psychiatric disorders and that works well in individuals with relatively well-formed selves but who suffer the consequences of excessive repression.

Unfortunately, individuals with more severe psychopathology failed to respond promptly to the classic approach; not only did they suffer symptoms arising as a result of repressed impulses, but also they were susceptible to the eruption of panic when threatened by a loss of self-cohesion. Object relations theory recognizes that the attachment to objects that are necessary to stabilize self-cohesion can be used as a paradigm not only for understanding severe psychopathology, but also for appropriately and therapeutically intervening with those patients.

The meaning of transference has also changed along the way. In the classical model, transference involved the displacement onto the analyst of unconscious repressed impulses. In self psychology, transference refers to the use of the selfobject of the analyst to repair deficits in the original self-selfobject representation. In object relations theory, trans-

ference refers to the use of the analyst as the primary object
for projective identifications; therefore, it incorporates the two
usages described above.

SUMMARY

Through general object relations theory, modern psychoanalysis integrates all previous psychoanalytic paradigms. It is true
that at the most primitive level we seek attachment and
support and suffer anxiety or depression when separated or
insufficiently mollified. At an intermediate level we seek
emotional closeness and intimacy, and we suffer narcissistic
injury in the absence of empathy, and anxiety as a result of
lost homeostasis in a state of self fragmentation. In more
developed individuals with better self-control, anxiety symptoms occur as a result of a threatened loss of control or the
sudden eruption of forbidden impulses and wishes.

Modern psychoanalysis can be considered to be object relations oriented because mental development certainly begins
as object oriented in the first place. Eventually the self built
upon those internal object relations assumes a considerable
degree of regulatory control, but it too requires feedback from
intimate objects. Modern psychoanalysis may also be considered ego psychology because even in the most autonomous
individuals sophisticated characterological defenses are still
necessary to manage repressed impulses associated with internal objects.

The modern psychoanalyst adjusts the frame of reference
and chooses the stance taken in analysis on the basis of the
organizational level of the individual in treatment. That such
divergent perspectives may be simultaneously operative occurs because of a fundamental human paradox.

On one hand man lives an individual existence. Each person
is born, is caught in time and dies. Each person has his own
experience of life and each of us lives in his own subjective
world pursuing personal pleasures and private fantasies, constructing a life which when his time is over will vanish. On
the other hand, people live necessarily and unavoidably

within a human community. The human infant can not survive without parental care. The most reclusive hermit thinks in language learned from others and experiences the world in categories influenced by early social relations. The human community and culture transcend the individual life span; in some sense the community creates the individual life, giving it substance and meaning. Man is essentially an individual animal and man is essentially a social animal. [Greenberg and Mitchell 1983, p. 400]

2

Faith

Faith is the substance of things hoped for and the evidence of things not seen.

—Hebrews 11:1

Although faith is a frequently encountered phenomenon it remains as yet an inexplicable experience in mental life. It can appear suddenly in the communications of our patients, and unfortunately is all too often passed over by us. Patients who profess to have strong religious beliefs and adhere to rigorous practices are often found to have little real faith, and others with little religious feeling can be strongly faithful. By and large, psychoanalysis has dealt with faith in theory only and has avidly avoided it in clinical practice. Therefore, to understand faith we will discuss how it may be derived from object relations, its association with character disorder, and the necessity for its growth in analysis.

Although faith and religion may be a somewhat unorthodox subject in a discussion of psychotherapy, how we came to it was rather straightforward. Firstly, regular contact with patients invariably presented instances in which the patient reported that it was mainly their religious belief and prayer that sustained them. Furthermore, as therapists we often seem to cross paths on medical and surgical wards with members of the clergy, especially when attending to patients who are terminally ill. In addition, we regularly encounter indi-

viduals who are long suffering, with severe character disorders, who may have failed a variety of different therapies, and
who are, nevertheless, able to find peace with God. Finally,
there is an interesting similarity between the struggle to
achieve emotional intimacy within the dyadic relationship in
psychotherapy and efforts to achieve communion with God,
so commonly expressed in exhortations to "trust in God" or
"walk with Jesus."

Before we continue with the body of the discussion of object relations and faith, we should say something else about
religious beliefs. Surveys of the general population reveal that
96 percent have a theistic orientation, whereas only 40 percent of psychiatrists and other scientists do (Angier 1997).
Among mental health professionals, those who are atheists
are more frequently found to have had psychoanalytic psychotherapy. The highest rate (40 percent) of apostasy—the
abandonment of the religious orientation in which a person
was reared—occurs among psychoanalysts. So, on one hand,
the general public appears to view and value religion as a
major element in their lives, especially during illness, death,
and dying, whereas on the other hand psychiatrists on the
whole do not. A number of studies indicate that the public
views psychiatrists as not knowing about and being unappre-
ciative of the important role of religion in their lives, whereas
many mental health professionals view the religious as naive, neurotic, or unsophisticated. Pastoral care therapists are
now rushing to fill the gap this disparity has created.

Most therapists have had the regular experience of their
most carefully crafted and exquisitely timed interpretations
falling on deaf ears, while other spontaneous comments or interactions produce profound reactions and precipitate break-
throughs to new states of awareness. It is as if growth (and
by extension cure), comes about to a significant degree in an
unpredictable, discontinuous fashion through some interaction with an unknown factor in the mind of the patient or in
the relationship with the analyst.

The same has been described with regard to the emergence

and the experience of faith. Considering the importance of faith in mental life for so many, it is noteworthy how psychoanalysis has distanced itself from the study of faith, and has dealt with it for the most part in theory only. According to Freud, religious ideas are "not the precipitates of experiences or end results of our thinking but illusions, fulfillment of the oldest, strongest and most urgent wishes of mankind. The secret of their strength lies in the strength of those wishes" (Freud 1927, p. 30). Although this is most certainly true with regard to most aspects of religion, it does not necessarily apply to the more important area of faith.

Following upon Freud in the American ego psychology school which has dominated psychoanalytic theory for much of the past fifty years, religious faith has been viewed as the outcome of the oedipal situation. It is a superego development whose aim is to deal with sexual and aggressive wishes. In it we recognize reaction formation; love for and submission to the beneficent God instead of hatred of the feared father, as well as compulsive rituals. In addition, we recognize the central role of biblical myths such as the near sacrifice of Isaac or the actual crucifixion of Christ, both of which involve fantasies of father–child murders (Mann 1962).

Following upon Klein in the British object relations school, Winnicott saw the evolving experience of self not so much as a defense against anxiety and the resolution of conflict, but as an original sense of joy and rapture in the movement from transitional object to object usage (Eigen 1981). Faith and its associated affects flow directly from this early developmental leap. Balint was also concerned about a "basic fault" that appeared in the psychopathology of his patients and that needed to be traversed in a leap in the analytic process (Balint 1968).

For Bion, faith is an even earlier mystical experience that begins in development as an absolute belief in an object called "O." It can be experienced but never known. He draws upon a distinction between *being* and *knowing,* states which, although inextricably linked, are qualitatively different (Eigen

1985). For Bion, the emotional truth in analysis turns on this point, and cure evolves out of this personal experience.

Although it is commonly believed outside psychiatry that faith plays an important role in healing, there is little agreement as to what that means, let alone how it occurs. Despite the recognition over the years that faith is an essential emotional state, there has been little formal application of it in psychoanalytic technique; nor has there been systematic investigation of its significance in bringing about cure. It is important to note, however, that the investigation of faith in this book will in no way support faith-healing, which, although distantly related, is not central to our discussion. Faith-healing often involves individuals who obtain cures or relief from disease through the direct and immediate effect of a magical religious-spiritual experience, or through participation in a wide variety of rituals—or just prayer. By contrast, the intent of our discussion is the examination of the role of faith in healing, but within the context of modern medicine and psychiatry, based on a biopsychosocial perspective of illness, and the ability of the physician to listen to and empathically understand the patient's suffering. It is the central assertion of this chapter that grief is fundamental to all illness, and that healing involves some quality of faith.

RELIGIOUS FAITH AND OBJECT RELATIONS

Martin Buber, a preeminent religious philosopher of the twentieth century, relates the following tale of the Hasidic Rabbi Shneur Zalman, of Northern White Russia, Belarus (who died in 1813). Rabbi Zalman was denounced to the authorities and ultimately executed. While in jail, he was approached by the chief of the gendarmes with the following question. "How are we to understand that God, the all-knowing, said to Adam 'Where art thou?' Didn't He know where his own creation was?" Rabbi Zalman answered the officer simply and directly that God's question: "Where art thou?" seeks to implore Adam to give an account of himself as to what he has been doing with his life, and how he has been hiding himself from the truth about himself. Rabbi Zalman continues to say that the question, although asked of Adam, is an eternal one, asking every man through every generation to examine the hideouts and falsehoods in his life and how he hides himself from the face of God. Adam's reply—"I was afraid and I hid myself"— is not so much a submission or surrender to authority as an examination of the truths about himself that allowed a re- turning to God (Buber 1966, pp. 9–10).

Buber goes on to say that the question by God is a pur- poseful effort to get Adam (and therefore, all men) to draw closer to God through the exploration of himself and the self-deceptions which pull him from his own true self.

How extraordinary a proposition it is—both Buber's and the Hasidic Rabbi's—that man's ills, no matter how complex, independent of psychology, social situation, or biological tem- perament, flow directly from his disconnection with God! And furthermore, that by giving an account of oneself and by be- ing able to say in effect "Here I am" one is able once again to become at peace with oneself and the world. It is this leap of faith and movement back to God (and therefore from a false to a true self) that leads to cure. In it we recognize an inter- esting overlap with object relations theory as directly applied in clinical practice.

No matter what theoretical framework one begins with or which particular aspects one prefers to emphasize, success- ful technique leads to an active drawing closer to the ana- lyst of the analysand, something that can be observed and felt directly, and by both parties, with the successive expres- sion of intense affects originally attached to the more primi- tive internal self objects (within the analysand). Are we not, therefore, in our asking our analysands for their associations, saying to them "Where art thou?" Are we not encouraging our patients to reveal themselves and their hideouts, to give a true account of themselves? And are patients not turning to us and allowing the emergence of their most intimate fears and feelings of shame when they admit "I was afraid and I was hiding"?

Returning to the Bible, in Genesis we discover that this
question by God to Adam is the first question that is asked
in the Bible, and that it is asked immediately after the eating of the fruit of the Tree of Knowledge. An alternative interpretation of this passage places God's question within the
context of Genesis itself, and speaks to another existential
position. According to the Talmud, consciousness and man's
awareness of self, just as in life itself, involve God's immediate presence, and it is God's activity through his question and
its penetration into his creation that brings forth consciousness. Consciousness itself, as an attribute existing only in
man, raises the question of its special origin, and it is argued
that it is God's intervention through his question that precipitates its awareness. Apparently eating fruit from the al-
legorical Tree of Knowledge was not in itself sufficient.

The passage in the Bible as it has been interpreted by rab-
binic scholars, therefore, speaks to two existential selves: one
that is experiential and relational, and the other that is more
observational and rational. In it, we recognize a similarity to
the duality of psychoanalytic technique, which moves at times
between the poles of neutral-interpretive observer and
empathic-introspective participants (Tuttman 1987).

According to Buber, although there are many variations
in the contents of faith, there are only two varieties of faith
(Buber 1951). Either one can have faith in someone else without knowing why one should have it, or else faith that something is true without knowing in fact that it is so. For the
theist, both varieties of faith coexist in the belief in a concept called God. Without factual evidence of its being so, the
theist both believes in God's continuous existence and trusts
in his beneficence. Although a believer may later maintain
rational-appearing "proofs" of his position, they never occur
a priori. God begins first in faith and is true regardless of
proof. In fact, if there were proof, it would no longer be faith.

Developmental theory postulates that the self, as distinct
from the object, arises as a direct outcome of multiple mother–
child interactions. By the middle of the second year of life the

infant normally completes a transition to toddler, wherein he/
she becomes more emotionally aware and makes greater use
of physical separateness. During this period, in Mahler's rapprochement phase, the child becomes even more aware that
the mother is not only a source of security but also a separate entity (Mahler et al. 1975). The child's interest and attention shift from locomotion and exploration to social interaction. Peek-a-boo games where the mother stimulates the
child by hiding and calling out "Where are you?" to the de-
light of the child are played over and over again. Basic trust
is the underlying relationship, and the individuating child
responds in time to the delightful and mysterious game of
peek-a-boo by hiding itself in turn and then announcing in
some fashion "here I am." It is remarkable that this game,
which reflects a milestone of self-object development, is so
reminiscent of the biblical question "Where art thou?" and the
response "I was hiding."

Faith, it would seem, begins in the earliest phases of individuation, long before there is any certain awareness of self
and obviously before any awareness of religion. Reason and
fact are relatively unimportant to the truth of faith and appear only as secondary elaborations to satisfy the needs of
rationality. The power of faith stems from its origins in the
early self–object relationship and many of its manifestations
(idealization, omnipotence, splitting), and its penetration
through the personality reflects this early beginning. Paul
Tillich, a preeminent protestant theologian, has stated that
"Faith as ultimate concern is an act of total personality. It
happens in the center of the personal life and includes all its
elements. Faith is the most centered act of the human mind"
(Tillich 1957, p. 3).

For the purposes of our thesis we will define faith as follows:

Faith is a state of self cohesion as a result of an arrangement of internal object relations that reflects the nature and
developing maturity of the combined observing and experiencing ego. It is a character structure that serves to main-

tain psychic stability at times of loss of stabilizing self/objects
by allowing for the transcendence of the immediate time and
local circumstances while continuing a state of interpersonal
connectedness. It may be externalized and directed to an idealized object, for example God, who may then assume qualities of infinite omnipresence. However, it does not require
such a projection or assignment, nor does it require objective
proof to be true.

What is novel about this conceptualization of faith is not
its parts but their arrangement. Faith does not require a
belief in God but does allow for one. The nature of that belief is related to the maturity of the ego and it may therefore
change over time and develop as a result of experience in or
outside of therapy. Secondly, it is a dynamic character structure that represents the developmental outcome of separation and individuation. It is not merely an infantile merger
experience of the kind described by Bion, and it may involve
much greater maturity than the transitional object usage of
Winnicott. It certainly involves a self observational component that goes beyond their formulations. Thirdly, as a character structure it serves as a stable set of defenses that especially come into play during periods of stress, conflict, or
serious loss. Lastly, it is a trust that endures over time and
physical separation. It enables a positive inner image of the
object to be sustained regardless of either satisfaction or disappointment, and it may undergo remodeling throughout a
lifetime in response to experiences of loss.

If there is an "illusion" to maintain, it is the illusion of object constancy. We currently think of object constancy as a
stable quantity that remains solid once it is achieved. But
object constancy, like faith, is a relative and fluid intrapsychic
state and often requires remodeling and the use of transitional objects, especially after periods of loss. Insofar as life
is filled with loss, the intense grief that we experience in
mourning may be in part the pain we suffer in giving up our
illusion of secure and constant objects and the emergence of
intense affects. Psychotherapy itself is commonly interrupted

by loss, with no other work being possible at the time of loss except the work of mourning (Tarachow 1963).

In the vast psychiatric literature on loss and grief there is little discussion concerning the appearance of faith. Yet so many of our patients have powerful, resurgent feelings of faith, including participation in religious rituals, at times of profound loss. Religious faith can serve as a means to restore the lost object (even everlastingly) as it softens the reality and allows the gradual mastery of loss. Melancholia, on the other hand, may be the despair and disorganization experienced with the collapse of faith and the inner sense of bitter and irredeemable abandonment.

Religion's association with object relations is especially manifest at times of loss or death. As an example, we will cite prayer from Reform Judaism's *New Union Prayer books*. It is a prayer for those who are facing death (in other words, all of us, someday), and it weaves together all threads of object relations: the question of what is truth, as well as the replacement of loss through creativity—all of which are contained within the concept of faith:

> Lord God of the Universe, creator of all that lives, although I pray for healing and continued life, still I know I am mortal. Give me the courage to accept whatever befalls me. The contemplation of my death should plant within my soul elevation and peace. Above all, it should make me see things in their true light. For all things which seem foolish in the face of death are really foolish in themselves. [*Gates of Prayer* 1975, p. 622]

> If only my hands were clean and my heart pure. But, alas, I have committed many wrongs and have left so much undone! And yet, I also know the good I did or tried to do. Let no one suppose that my smallest act of goodness was wasted for society at large. All our help, petty though it be, is needed, and though we know not the manner, the fruit of every faithful service is gathered in. May that goodness then impart an eternal meaning to my life.

Lord God, protector of the helpless, watch over my loved ones in whose souls my own is knit. For You are the divine source of mercy and truth. Into your hands I commend my spirit. My body and spirit are yours and in your presence I cast off fear and am at rest. [Stem 1977, p. 128]

What is more, the concept of worship has also been elucidated:

Worship is more than an act of cognition; it is a turning of the whole being toward that which we affirm as ultimately real and valuable. Humble in the face of a reality whose essence we can not "Know," we speak in metaphors. Our "truth" is a truth of the heart no less than of the mind. The "facts" we assert are the facts of a hopeful spirit. But we believe that the spiritual reality within us corresponds to a spiritual reality beyond us, and in worship we hope to bring the two realities into communion. [*Gates of Prayer* 1975, p. xi]

Everything we have been trying to delineate with regard to faith is included in this prayer and metaphor of worship. We note a loving trust while transcending the ultimate loss. We hear of joining and communion instead of separation and isolation. One can feel a movement toward acceptance and peace instead of confusion and anxiety. We are told about truth and facts. Obviously not objective facts, but truths nevertheless. And we notice a focus on an elevated sense of caring, and concepts of mercy and forgiveness, instead of on judgment and punishment. Although couched in religious terms, and in relation to a godlike being, the sentiments are certainly understandable and do not require a god to be true. Everyone would prefer to face their own demise with the acceptance and generosity of spirit contained in this prayer rather than the fear and helplessness that so commonly occur; and if one resonates with the hopes of the prayer, does that make one religious or theistic?

Faith—and the sense of secure joining that accompanies it—is a reflection of the love obtained from "good-enough" objects. Having good-enough objects allows the stabilizing organization of faith, which protects the differentiating self from crippling disorganization. Disorganized, pathological characters, on the other hand, are distrustful, and have limited ability to master their anxious feelings appropriately via either transcending imagination or verbalization; instead, they act out or become symptomatic. Good-enough objects allow for verbalization, flexibility, and imaginative creativity of new objects at times of loss, activities whose purpose is to join and reconnect us. The objects created are modified and crafted with the passage of time and are internalized when they are so personally worked upon. The successful imaginative creation of internal objects that are loving and sustaining is the bedrock of faith. According to Pollock, "creative work or play is only found when there has been a successful mourning process" (Pollock 1978, p. 263). Consequently, in the process of seeking transcendence over the immediate experience, the self is continuously being reshaped and remolded (Jaspers 1959).

PSYCHODYNAMIC TECHNIQUE AND FAITH

In therapy one must examine the discrepancy between the religiosity of the patient and the maturity of the underlying faith. Brief examples of such examination from the therapy of religious individuals include the following. One Hasidic woman with inflammatory bowel disease stated quite early in therapy that she felt God hated her. Over time, she was observed to have numerous histrionic traits and regularly abused drugs. After several years of testing and acting out, a history of sexual molestation by her siblings was uncovered. In another case, an elderly Catholic woman with a family tree filled with nuns and priests stated that God had abandoned her. She had lost her son at a young age and had never resolved the loss. She was chronically enraged and felt betrayed by God. She prayed directly to her son whom she substituted for Jesus, the "son of God." On the other hand, a neurotically anxious Catholic woman who converted and married a Moslem man felt that God was one and the same and loved her however she referred to or named him, but also was very attached to her father and unable to give him up while remaining only minimally attached to her husband.

In each of these examples, a deeper examination of the nature of the patients' faith, beyond their religious beliefs and practices, provided early important clues about the state of their conflicts and relationships to important objects. As is often the case, although they present themselves as long suffering by the hand of God, they struggle with intense feelings of guilt about their unconscious drives (Renik 1991).

An explanation with regard to the nature of faith is especially of value in those patients with severe character pathology of the narcissistic or borderline type. Faith is not so easily elicited from these individuals and it is very fragile. Patients of this kind often express a sense of void within, "like being in a deep pit or black hole." In it they feel completely alone, and isolated or with feelings of nothingness or chaos (Chessick 1995). They report that when they leave the session they feel as if you, the caring therapist, have disappeared completely. They resort to addictions and habitual hostile clinging behaviors to blunt the pain of the emptiness that they feel. They act out, are self-destructive, and make emergency calls to force your return and attention. They often admit that they don't trust anybody and have little real faith in themselves. As the therapist actively engages and empathically tries to understand the patient's painful inner experience, the void is transiently filled with the object of the therapist. The repeated experience of trusting another human being while simultaneously working through and testing them with projective identifications enables the patient to solidify a faith in the continuous existence of the relationship with the therapist and ultimately, therefore, in a synthetic sense of self. In the end, effective treatment and healing is always associated with a restoration of faith for these people. Ultimately, the void in these individuals can only be filled by a faith in a durable, trustworthy object, hopefully one encountered in therapy.

If faith is a necessary outcome of treatment and central to healing, how do we promote faith in therapy, especially in those who have so little—and especially if we do not want to proselytize? Only "empathic listening" can create the milieu for its development, and the good listener is the best physician for those who are ill in thought and feeling (Johnson 1992). If it is assumed that the central defect in severe character disorder is the lack of sufficient empathy in early development, because of neglect, excessive intrusion, or even overt abuse, then it becomes apparent that empathy again provided by the object (now in the person of the participating analyst) can serve to restore the defect, and begin the healing through the restoration of faith and interpersonal connectedness.

In therapy, when we observe sudden and dramatic flights into health, we know them to be defensive positions behind which lie frightening if not overwhelming affects. They frequently account for the impasses in negative therapeutic reactions (Danielian 1988). Individuals so affected are under enormous tension; their defenses are unstable and often deteriorate over time. In many ways they are similar to individuals who have sudden religious conversions; they must be treated quite gently.

A breach of faith occurring, even unintentionally, as a result of an interruption of empathic listening on the part of the psychiatrist leads to injury and an increased sense of isolation for the patient. It inevitably leads to acting out, noncompliance, or a resistance to further work in therapy until the breach is traversed. The aggression that emerges from these patients with poor impulse control is intended either as a direct retaliation for the injury that has been sustained or as a means to signal the analyst to proceed carefully so as to prevent any further disruption and disconnection. The absence of faith or the threat of its loss is therefore a significant cause for the emergence of aggression.

We know that susceptible individuals who perceive a challenge to their religious system, either psychologically, socially, or politically, will regress to and act out, within a socially sanctioned group process, the most extraordinary evil, including acts of brutality and violence, all of which are of course committed in the name of God. They may have an intense conviction with regard to their beliefs but it is hardly faith in any sense that we have been discussing here. Evil is not merely characterological, maladaptive, irrationally destructive behavior. Nor does evil occur merely as a result of the influence of an external omnipotent "Satan." Evil is the sadistic pleasure enjoyed in the deliberate effort to aggressively control and then destroy the loved and hated object. Evil evolves where faith has been corrupted.

Case History

D. is a 27-year-old white female who presented with complaints of incapacitating pelvic pain and depression. She was the second of two children raised in a strictly Orthodox Jewish family. Her father was a tailor, her mother was a Holocaust survivor, and her older brother is a physician.

The patient's upbringing was intense and conflicted. She described her mother as cold, austere, and long-suffering, never offering a compliment or a hug, and continuously absorbed in work and the ordeals of day-to-day life, and her father as lively, clever, fun-loving, but overly affectionate physically. She admitted to volunteering for sexual play with a group of similar-age girls in which objects were inserted into her vagina by the oldest participant. This occurred at age 5.

The patient stated that she had little awareness of herself or the world as a child. She attended an all-girls strictly orthodox yeshiva and was completely compliant with all authority, rules, prohibitions, and rituals. She had little sense of being either intelligent or physically attractive, and in fact she felt the opposite.

At age 19 the patient married an Orthodox man and dropped out of college to begin raising a family. Sex was unprotected, occurred only with ritual postmenstrual immersion and after the proscribed waiting period, and was seldom pleasurable or orgasmic. The patient's husband became a successful currency trader and provided for an extremely luxurious lifestyle. Although a good provider and a very decent, honorable, and Orthodox man, he was nevertheless emotionally distant and physically inhibited. He was also compulsively preoccupied with hand-washing, lock-checking, and religious rituals.

The patient, craving physical affection and constant emotional reassurance, sought out other men for compliments and interest. Beginning with her best friend's husband, she underwent a transformation that culminated in an extramarital affair with a physician who was middle-aged and unattached. Shortly thereafter the patient had the first onset of severe pelvic pain that progressed in severity until, over the next nine months, she became completely incapacitated.

When she was finally referred for psychiatric treatment (only after the insistence of her lover), she was found to not only have a chronic pelvic-pain syndrome but also major depression with marked suicidal intent. In addition, she was quite histrionic and hypochondriacal. The patient entered into treatment with the permission of her husband for the overt purpose of helping her with her pelvic pain, but it was rapidly clear that she was seeking to be rescued from the extramarital affair that threatened to destroy her marriage, leading to disgrace and total abandonment. The initial phase of analysis consisted almost entirely of dramatic complaints of pain in the lower abdomen, with exaggerated expressions of suffering. She sought referrals from many physicians, gynecologists, physical therapists, chronic pain specialists, and others who recommended a multitude of different approaches, all of which failed to resolve the pain but which led to a state of confusion and helplessness.

This early phase of analysis was marked by rigidity and distrust. The patient complained frequently of pain but

smugly reacted to all efforts to help her with statements
to the effect that nobody could—least of all the analyst.
She offered the opinion, which was supported by family
and friends, that therapy was an easy way to steal her
money by preying on her helplessness and dependency.
Furthermore, she suggested that the analyst too would
take advantage of her separation anxiety and never will-
ingly let her leave treatment. The patient admitted to
being distrustful of others and knew that in most instances
she could manipulate most people either with money or
seductive behavior. She stated that she did not trust the
analyst nor, for that matter, could she trust herself. She
had little faith in anything or anybody. Although she was
religiously orthodox she felt that God hated her. Although
her belief in God was immediate, her faith in Him was
quite limited. Nevertheless she was fearful that analysis
would subvert her religiosity. Despite her outward physical attractiveness she had an ugly self-image, with a poorly
differentiated body image. In her view, her mind, internal
physical functions, and outward physical appearance were
all significantly deficient. She had little faith in herself.

Slowly connections were made between the patterns of
her childhood and the present. She was able to recognize
feelings of rage with her parents, especially her mother,
and her guilt too, because her mother was a long-suffering Holocaust survivor. She was able to see the connection
between her mother's aloofness and her husband's, as well
as the connection between her childhood sexual excitations
and later inhibitions and sexual acting out. She also voiced
many feelings of guilt with regard to her anger with her
mother, her father's preferential treatment of her, and her
betrayal of her husband.

The middle phase of analysis progressed more smoothly,
with substantial improvements noted in her physical and
social activity. Therapy focused more deeply on her poor
self-image and her distrust and lack of faith in herself as
well as her intense drive to obtain seemingly powerful

external objects to secure her. It was during this period that the patient encountered the intensity of an erotic transference that erupted in the analysis. Despite her fear and her urges to run from analysis, she was able to tolerate her rage at the analyst and suffer the disappointment of not having her sexual desires gratified. This transferential experience resulted in greater self-esteem, as a result of greater control of her impulses, which in turn resulted in greater trust in herself in conducting herself in interpersonal relationships. She now for the first time developed a more confident sense of her intelligence as well as a more realistic appreciation of her self-worth.

When the analysis entered the termination phase, the patient struggled through the usual regression and symptomatic return but then, after nine months of struggle with her fear of separation, offered the following just prior to leaving:

"When I first came to you I had lost faith in God because of my father's death. I felt that He had abandoned me. But now my faith is restored. It is as if you became my rabbi. I am more lenient with religious observance than I used to be but I do not feel as guilty, and I am more forgiving of myself. I am more comfortable with what I feel is truly important for me. I feel closer to God now than I ever did and I believe again. Because of analysis I have found faith. It is as if when I felt that God had completely abandoned me, He in fact delivered me to you of all people, an apparently non-religious individual, to help me resurrect my faith. To Him, and to you, I give thanks."

FAITH'S ROLE IN HEALING

Physical and mental diseases are most often thought of as physiological or pathological derangements that can be observed at the level of cells, tissues, organs, or physiological systems. Illness, on the other hand, is generally thought of as the entire bio-psycho-social response to the disease state, including interpersonal behaviors as well as psychological responses. A similar distinction can be made between cure and healing. Where cure may refer to the resolution of disease, healing more broadly involves the resolution of illness. In fact, one of the more specific meanings of healing is "to make whole," and for our purposes here we will limit our discussion to this more special meaning of healing, that is, to create union and to make whole.

Although little effort has been made to formalize any approach to illness or healing in medicine and psychiatry, we regularly encounter patients in emotional turmoil that is disproportionate to the extent or magnitude of the disease, with pathological grief responses that require healing obtained from a treatment apart from the cure of their disease.

When ill, patients first and foremost seek cures, to restore their physical intactness and health to whatever extent possible. They will make extraordinary efforts to avoid loss or to restore themselves to the state they experienced before the loss of health. But since disease and physiological derangements are beyond an individual's control, they will seek restoration from outside themselves and turn to those who provide hope and cure. It is in those persons that patients often place faith, according to their psychological and cultural milieu. Because of the presence of loss and the regression to earlier states that it induces, patients who are acutely injured are likely to resort to splitting and idealize the ones in whom they have faith, usually their physicians. Even before the actual treatment of the disease, healing begins with the faith that is invested in the projected idealized objects. Often the more simple and open the faith, the more quickly the healing begins.

Trust and security undoubtedly also lead to physiological changes that may directly affect the course of *disease* states, and may even at times bring about cure. However, more importantly, faith's effect of making one feel whole psychologically and thereby able to transcend the disorganization of loss always leads to dramatic changes in *illness* behavior. There is a rapid decline in anxiety and obsessive rumination and a decrease in somatic complaints and clinging, as well as improved energy and quality of sleep while other biological treatments begin to take effect on the disease state.

It is unsurprising, therefore, that studies of the effects of placebos show that placebos account for upwards of 30 percent of the statistically significant change. Faith is even more powerful with respect to psychiatric disorders (e.g., schizophrenia, bipolar disorder, obsessive-compulsive disorder, etc.) because in addition to suffering the pain of the symptoms from the biological condition with which they are afflicted, due to the immediate impact on psychological function, the individuals also suffer the pain of disruption of loss of faith in themselves.

The significance of faith in healing can be inferred from another type of evidence, more obvious but still somewhat indirect. Faith is most commonly discussed in relation to religion, and the role of religion in healing is an ancient, universal theme. As mentioned earlier, the overwhelming majority of patients have a religious and spiritual orientation, and if they are to be healed they must be listened to and understood from within their own frame of reference (Tucker 1989). Furthermore, most individuals expect that religion and prayer are important aids to their healing (Coleman 1991).

Recently, religious coping has been more formally studied and has been demonstrated to be helpful with illness. In a large population survey of 92,000 individuals, those who attended religious services once or more per week had over a 50 percent reduction in death from a variety of diseases. There was also a 53 percent decline in the incidence of suicide (*Clinical Psychiatric News* 1996). Among the elderly ill, religious coping has been found to be inversely related to depression (Koenig et al. 1992). Reliance on spiritual and/or religious belief systems has also been demonstrated to reduce distress in coping with cancer (Sis et al. 1992, p. 24). Furthermore, religious beliefs and practices were commonly found among psychiatric inpatients and again found to be inversely correlated with depression and anxiety disorders (Kroll and

Sheehan 1989). Since anxiety and depressive states involve a sense of isolation and disconnection, these findings are consistent with our earlier stated proposition about the interpersonal nature of faith. Those who have faith are less likely to feel disconnected and therefore less likely to suffer affective disorders.

Conversely, it is also true that those who are hopeless and without faith suffer greater illness, morbidity, and even death (Jenkins 1996). The characteristics of hopelessness include a sense of doom, the end, of being "finished"; but, more importantly, because the patient has little faith in others, he or she assumes all responsibility for the result, with a personal sense of failure and self-denigration following his or her incapacity to shape the course of events. Of course underlying the conscious thoughts and surface feelings are latent feelings of abandonment, rage, and wishes for revenge. As a result, such persons retreat further from support from the world, and that increases an already elevated state of internal physiological dysregulation leading to increased stress and worsening of their illness.

With regard to psychotherapeutic technique, one can simply inquire, when it is appropriate, if the patient does on occasion pray. Most individuals answer in the affirmative. One can follow the response by requesting that the patient share the content of his or her recent prayers with you. It is amazing what people will say and for what they have prayed—the answers are invariably revealing. Patients may at times ask the therapist to pray with them, or assume that the therapist shares similar beliefs. Such convictions can be handled like any other transference interaction. Questions about why an individual believes in God are generally not psychologically productive; there are too many intellectual abstractions offered as justification for particular beliefs. But, if the subject of religion does comes up, one might inquire as to whether the patient is religious, and if so, how they imagine their personal relationship with God. A patient who, for example, informs you that he is religious but God hates him, tells you that you have a very troubled individual on your hands.

For borderline patients and others with severe character disorders, after some time in treatment at an appropriate point an inquiry can be made about whom they have faith in. Predictably they will say "Nobody." It is then appropriate to ask them, "Do you mean you don't believe in yourself either?" They will usually say "No." If you then ask whether they have faith in you, they will respond with something to the effect of: "I'm not sure," or, "Not really," or "Why should I?"—to which one might answer: "Why not, and if not me then whom, and if not now then when?" What ultimately appears is a fundamental distrust and fear of taking a chance and having faith in the other and therefore in themselves. The question for which there *is* no answer is: "How do I make this leap of faith?" No one knows the answer to that one—only that "they must"!

In general, there is permeability and overlap between the reliance upon religious healing and psychotherapy. Whereas psychotherapy relies on a system of mind and body, religious healing is tripartite in nature, including mind, body, and spirit (Csordas 1990). Religious healing relies on an externalized concept of spirit beyond mind and body, whereas for modern western science and psychiatry, the spiritual is but a special existential domain yet incorporated within the psychological realm. Although the object of transcendence is more readily identified for the theist (namely God), the same spiritual quest is necessary for the atheist. For both, it is in the transcendence of faith through which inner emptiness and fragmentation are bridged (Nino 1990). Religious belief in God and in the power of prayer, however, is only one of many possible belief systems. Studies comparing a variety of belief systems in coping with illness seem to indicate that it is not the type of belief so much as the flexibility of the system that leads to best outcome, just as flexibility is important in good parenting. Religious devotion, but not conservatism or rigidity, improves the coping with stress (Kendler 1997).

The issue thus is not the content of the individual belief system but the nature of the underlying faith. Where religious faith appears in psychotherapy (and it frequently does), paying attention to the associated affects and object relations is far more revealing than focusing on the nature of its contents or rituals. For theists, an open, expansive, and loving vision of God is entirely different from the idea of a punitive and merciless being whom the patient feels must hate them unless they conform to a rigid set of rules. Furthermore, in clinical practice one observes that the more rigidly and stridently a belief system is held, the weaker is the faith of the one who holds it, despite all the rhetoric. A person of deep intrinsic faith feels connected even during illness or after object loss and is adaptive as well as forgiving. Those with limited faith, or who demand submission to a system of rigid extrinsic control are in turn demanding and controlling, and distrustful and hateful of others. At times of loss or helplessness they are more likely to cope poorly and to suffer increased affective disturbance because of their feeling of being disconnected. And of course they are deeply hostile and destructive.

When religious faith emerges in therapy, a more vigorous examination of the affect (what it feels like and not necessarily the nature of its content or rituals) can lead to valuable understanding as to the unconscious conflicts and deficits within the internal object relations. Furthermore, most patients have a theistic orientation and expect that religion will be of help to them.

Religion has indeed too often in the past been associated with superstitious beliefs about causality, beliefs that make it unacceptable as an explanatory paradigm in the nature of illness or healing. This is especially true with regard to the mentally ill who until only recently were considered to be under the influence of demons. The role of religion in medicine and psychiatry has not always been a noble one.

Freud's classical system of drives (id) is similar to the first-cause theories in philosophy and is related to Fichte's *Ich* (Durant 1961) as well as Nietzsche's will to power in *Gene-*

alogy of Morals (1887) and the biology inherent in Darwin's *The Origin of Species* (1859). In the classic schema, drives power a biologically bounded neurological system which only later, in ego psychology, is organized into the mechanistic psychic apparatus of defense and conflict. Only after Freud could the theory be lifted entirely out of the biological frame of reference into the dualistic world of object relations. Freud, however, clearly preferred the scientific frame of reference for his theory and the rational method presumed to exist within the neutral observer. His considerable efforts in this regard have given rise to a consensually valid system of mind that is ongoing even as it competes with rapid advances in biological brain sciences and neuropsychology. But Freud's disdain of the irrational, subjective beliefs inherent in religion is perhaps the major reason for the avoidance by the psychoanalytic community of a more thorough exploration of faith.

Ernest Jones has stated that Freud "grew up devoid of any belief in God or immortality and does not appear to have felt a need for it" (Jones 1956a, p. 465). Even Freud referred to himself as a godless Jew. Although Freud was in fact a man who was concerned with morality, ethics, and honor, he himself could not explain why he should care to have been so. Freud appears to have been conversant with all Jewish customs and festivals, despite being an atheist. Although his children were not familiar with Jewish religious traditions (Gay 1988), throughout his adult life Freud was certainly preoccupied with religion (Jones 1956b, pp. 372–373) and maintained a membership in B'nai B'rith. For thirty years he also maintained a very close personal tie to and a strong identification with the Swiss pastor Oskar Pfister, and in his later years wrote him the following letter after a period of illness:

Dear Dr. Pfister,

After another major operation I am fit for a little and uncheerful but, if I have got back some kind of synthesis again by the end of the month—that is what I have been promised—

am I to miss the opportunity of seeing my old but by *God's* grace rejuvenated friend here? Certainly not, I count on it.

Cordially yours, Freud [Meng 1963, p. 137, italics added]

Of course this in no way suggests theism on Freud's part; but it does demonstrates a personal closeness and respect for his dear friend who happened to be a clergyman.

The issue of Freud's relationship to religion and his beliefs regarding it is of relevance because with regard to faith, as Fromm has rightfully pointed out, "unfortunately the discussion, centered around religion since the days of the Enlightenment, has been largely concerned with affirmation or negation of certain human attitudes" (Fromm 1950, p. 133). "Do you believe in God?" has been the crucial question of religionists, and the denial of God has been the position chosen by those fighting the church. But it is easy to see that many who profess a belief in God are, in their human attitude, idol worshipers filled with hate and without faith, while some of the most ardent "atheists," devoting their lives to the betterment of mankind and to deeds of brotherliness and love, have exhibited faith and a profoundly religious attitude (Fromm 1950).

Freud, it would seem, was an example of such an "unbelieving" man, and it is reasonable to conclude that part of his motivation in his constant creative struggle and in his preoccupation with Moses was, among other things, an effort to maintain a close identification with and a tie to the faith of his father.

SUMMARY

We have tried to demonstrate that in order to understand religion we first must recognize the nature of the underlying object relations, which are the building blocks of faith. This, however, should not be understood as a blanket endorsement of theism or religion, and particularly not of their dogmatic and compulsively submissive forms. But clearly, psychoanalysis and psychotherapy, a century after their inception, need to address the centrality of faith in development and cease to negate its importance to patients. Insofar as faith is an outgrowth of early development, it must be fundamental to the self, and as a uniquely human experience deserves as much attention in our analytic work and understanding of object relations as other concepts ordinarily receive. The reason religion and God are so important to many is because of the enormous power and self-sustaining subjective truth emanating from faith. Although subjective in nature, this experience of truth is as powerful and persuasive as the consensually validated objective truths of science, and often as long-lived. As an outgrowth of early development and character structure it must be fundamental to the self. Clearly those without faith, even if they are "religious," suffer continuously between the rock of anxiety and the hard place of emptiness. Faith, as we have tried to demonstrate, is essential to restoring a state of wholeness, and therefore of healing.

Although historically theologians have a claim to the area of faith, psychotherapy is consistent with a universalist ecumenism and humanistic tolerance of religious pluralism and has much to say about faith as an essential component of character structure. Both psychoanalysts and theologians in their own way seek truth and meaning and in so doing strive for the highest in human attainment. Both also seek to understand aggression and the means to prevent its unwarranted expression, for it is also true that the threat of a loss of faith invariably leads to an inner sense of despair and hopelessness, and consequently continues to be of prime importance with regard to aggression in or outside of therapy. However, we do differ in that, for the theologian, religious faith in God is the primary goal and the only important aspirational object in life, while in psychoanalysis, faith is the eventual outcome of the extensive work done within the relationship, and it can neither be created by making it the prime focus, nor is a God necessary as its prime object.

Finally, with regard to morality and ethics, and why we

should be governed by them, philosophical thought through the ages has generally affirmed that ethics and morality are an adaptive intellectual process and therefore preferable if not beneficial to mankind. Theologians stand on more level intellectual ground in their personal belief and assertions that ethics and morality are simply divinely inspired. It is our view that ethics and morality are so powerful and motivating because they are not only a humane interpersonal process but also because they are faith-inspired. In our opinion, the deeper the faith the more profound are the ethical considerations, and the more deeply motivated is the moral action. Since we psychiatrists have special obligations with regard to the inclusion of ethical deliberations in our clinical work as well as in our communication with our colleagues, we must examine the nature of our own faith within our work before we can really guide our medical colleagues.

We have tried to demonstrate that faith is at the core of our work and organized by the internal object relations, and that it is important to recognize both these aspects in our patients and ourselves. Is it not time, also, to recognize that we live in a house of faith, and to stop acting as if we are just visitors because we do not identify with all our religious neighbors? After a hundred years of clinical practice and theory, is it not time to settle in and recognize this house of faith as our own?

3
Body Image

As Gregor Samsa awoke one morning from uneasy
dreams, he found himself transformed in his bed into a
giant insect.
—Franz Kafka, *The Metamorphosis*

INTRODUCTION

Understanding the role of faith is fundamental to psychotherapy because the ultimate aim of our work is the alleviation of suffering. Unfortunately, the restoration of faith alone
may not be sufficient. Pain and suffering are most commonly
experienced within the body and they activate psychological
conflicts and defenses related to the body image. Therefore,
to effectively heal our patients and relieve suffering in psychotherapy, we need to further develop an understanding of
the role of object relations in illness behavior and in the formation of the body image. Then we will be able to discuss
the natural convergence of body and soul in object relations.

In general, psychoanalytic practice has been so uncomfortable with the psychological meaning of body image that almost all our theory of mind has been lifted entirely out of the
physical realm of the body. We have made the transition from
the accommodation of instinctual drives through the adaption
of ego psychology to the purely psychological realms of object relations. But the corporal body has been left behind! The
notion that the mind is firstly immersed in the body is as old-

fashioned as drive theory. Today, we are more comfortable with the concepts of projective identification, acting out, and negative therapeutic reactions.

Furthermore, even when we talk about the life cycle, it is almost exclusively with respect to psychosocial developmental tasks that are either attained or incompletely dealt with at specific phases of life. Ordinarily we don't consider illness as among the normal phases of the life cycle, yet whose life is without major illness? Perhaps we are inclined not to consider illness within the normal developmental process because it is related primarily to the body, and its occurrence is so variable and to a large extent unpredictable. And perhaps also because illness is so ego dystonic, unwanted, and seemingly inflicted upon us unfairly from outside our own being.

But what about the old concept of body image: How does it apply in today's object-relations theory? What are its implications for psychoanalytic technique? How relevant is it for understanding behavior during periods of illness, and how is a positive body image necessary for alleviating suffering? I am reminded of at least three psychoanalysts I treated, for various time frames, two of whom were training analysts. They all reacted to their ordinary illnesses with statements to the effect of "I never thought that anything like this would ever happen to me." There was the wounded narcissism of a psychological self that felt that it could pass through life intact without being affected by insults to the physical or mental self.

How we cope with and adapt to illness, or even how we manage at the end of our lives, often has more to do with our body image as derived from the interplay of object relations during the first three years of life, rather than at any other point in the life cycle. In these early years before the full psychological emergence of the self, with the capacity for self-observation, the internal self is regulated by interactions with and a developing faith in the security of its object relations. The newborn infant (and later the toddler) is secured and soothed by ministrations of others in the outside world. Cries of hunger, coldness, fatigue, and all other internal sensations are mediated by comfort and touch from the mother or father. We organize our inner sensations—which crystalize into a sense of self—through direct contact with our real objects. Conversely, changes in or the absence of those caring objects leads to dysregulation of internal sensations and abnormality of expressions that ultimately result in what have been referred to in the past as psychosomatic diseases, not to mention effects on other aspects of our developing character.

When they are ill, adults often behave like the children they once were and reenact early object relations. Conversely, in the very young, illness is often deeply associated with the psychological self. The child so afflicted feels that if they are ill it must be that they have been or are "bad" in a global sense. They feel that they are being punished, for some reason related to projections arising from within their own world of object relations.

BODY IMAGE AND PSYCHOSOMATICS

Body image is not only the perception of one's body, but also the emotional significance attached to its various physical parts (Goin and Goin 1981). These include surface appendages and contours, inner sensations and functions, as well as its outer space and boundaries. Freud (1923), in reference to the body image, described the ego as "first and foremost a body ego; it is not merely a surface entity but itself the projection of surface" (p. 26).

Schilder, in his 1935 classic *The Image and Appearance of the Human Body*, extended the body image concept beyond an individual's psychological investment in the body or its parts and the perception of its appearance and sensations to a psychological unity that is incorporated and reflects the sum total of internal sensations and interpersonal relationships. Greenacre (1958) stated that the body image is the core both of the incipient ego and of the later self-image, and that the body areas that are most significant are the face and the genitals.

The individual organizes his body image through the integration of multiple perceptions and interactions with primary objects beginning with the earliest stages of development (Kolb 1959, Mahler and McDevitt 1982). The infant is an open rather than a closed homeostatic system; it responds profoundly, both acutely and chronically, to the threat of separation from the powerful psychophysiological regulators of intimately securing objects (Taylor 1992). Although the child independently explores the environment and actively practices with his or her body to develop a sense of his or her skills, both physical and mental, these explorations and experiences all occur within an approximate relationship to the primary object. Just as a sense of good or bad self depends upon that relationship to the object, so also does the differentiation of the body self and the mental self although these are as yet only minimally developed. In addition, autonomous and stable self-physiological regulatory control only occurs with maturation and the development of stable internal objects. Even so, throughout life even autonomous individuals require external objects to maintain internal homeostasis, physical or mental.

Individuals who experienced conflicts at an early age with objects that were overwhelming and associated with heightened states of arousal, pain, or anxiety, may also have suffered physiological dysregulation, which often leads, later in life, to psychosomatic disturbances (Taylor 1992). Dysregulated physiological states in a susceptible infant and alterations in arousal would in time affect perceptions of physical sensation such as touch and smell, muscular tension (such as chest tightness), internal sensations (such as bowel and bladder fullness), the perception of pain, and the general orientation to objects (i.e., clinging or apathy) (Kernberg 1984). It is the common clinical experience with individuals with psychosomatic disorders or who are otherwise disease-prone—patients with chronic pain syndromes or other physiologically dysregulated disorders—that they often manifest severely disturbed object relations and resemble individuals with borderline and narcissistic personality disorders (Taylor 1987). These individuals offer complaints of multiple symptoms and invariably have a negative body image. There are often associated high rates of co-morbidity, and a family history of affective disorder. The efforts most of these patients make to focus on their physical condition or disease are often at the cost of masking the underlying deficits in internal object relations, which are rigidly defended and rapidly come into play when confronted in therapy. A 35-year follow-up study of healthy college undergraduates demonstrated higher lifetime incidence of physical illness in those individuals who initially reported lower scores in ratings of parental caring (Russek and Schwartz 1997).

It is not surprising that sudden changes in body parts, even many years later during periods of illness and regression, can elicit states of anxiety related to fears of separation, abandonment, or a damaged or disintegrated self. Conversely, anxiety can give rise to distorted perceptions of change in the body's integrity that are out of keeping with reality (E. Kafka 1971).

Case History

P., a 50-year-old married white female, presented herself one month after post resection of a tongue carcinoma and radiotherapy to the lower jaw and neck. The patient presented with complaints of depression, including hopelessness, helplessness, poor concentration, social isolation, tearfulness, poor sleep, early morning anxiety, anhedonia, and poor appetite. She had been informed that, from a medical-surgical standpoint, her prognosis was excellent. She had a mild residual speech defect but was not emotionally prepared to engage in speech therapy. As a result of radiotherapy she was experiencing some dryness and a decrease in taste discrimination. In addition she had erythema of the skin of the lower jaw and neck with induration that accentuated her normal skin folds.

The patient was overwhelmed by her grief and depression and was angry that she had developed cancer at such a young age. She was preoccupied by the perceived change in her physical appearance and was excessively self-conscious of her speech defect. She no longer felt sexually desirable. Ordinarily a meticulously groomed person, she found the changes in her physical appearance disgusting and overwhelming. Whereas previously she took enormous pride in her relatively youthful appearance she now felt old and ugly. In the mirror she saw herself as a woman of 70 instead of the 40 she formerly imagined. Finally, although her surgeon and family recommended minor cosmetic surgery she steadfastly refused because she was unable to cope with the prospect of further procedures.

Initially, treatment was begun with interpersonal psychotherapy, with the prime focus on the impact on family role function of her having cancer and the changes in her appearance and speech. She made an excellent recovery over several months, with the resolution of all her depressive symptoms, and was able to eliminate her speech defect through involvement in speech therapy. Nevertheless, as a result of radiation she had a permanent change in skin turgor of the neck which left the area appearing considerably aged. The patient, although medically recovered, reported that she felt considerably older. Her husband and family were quite pleased by her appearance, did not see the need for any further psychological treatment, and were just delighted that she was no longer ill. The patient, however, felt unalterably disfigured, and experienced chronic anxiety and emotional turbulence around her body image. She remained self-conscious of the appearance of her neck and continued to feel unattractive and undesirable.

A switch was then made to psychodynamic psychotherapy, in which her body image was the center of focus; soon the patient chose to undergo minor cosmetic surgery. One month later she reported that she felt entirely well, energetic, and satisfied. She felt that she once again looked like her former youthful self and now approximated her age as being in the mid-forties. Her appearance once again approximated her internal body image with which she was happy.

It was noteworthy that, although the surgery provided only moderate improvement in cosmesis, it precipitated a far more dramatic transformation in body image and internal self-worth. Only after the cosmetic surgery did the patient recognize the deeper value she placed on physical attractiveness and the role it played in early childhood in competing with her mother and two sisters for her father's affection as his favorite.

Although a person's perceptions of body image undergo continual evolution throughout the life cycle, this usually occurs at the preconscious level. A sudden or overwhelming change in the body through illness can superimpose itself on earlier experiences of bodily change that were painful or conflict-ridden to initiate a depression (Peto 1972) or activate a psycho-physiological disease. According to Taylor, "Many childhood and adult diseases may be conceptualized as disorders of regulation, and the onset of illness sometimes has the adaptive effect of restoring an important interpersonal relationship which is relied upon for its psychobiological regulatory functions" (Taylor 1987, p. 167).

Ultimately, ego stabilization and adaptation after illness involve a process of reintegration of the body image. An adequately recrafted body image, though never perfect, may nevertheless be sufficiently adaptive for the patient. Therefore, the underlying body image must always be a part of the work in analysis. When asked casually, a patient who is suffering, from whatever cause, will typically respond to the question of "How do you feel?" with: "Old." But, when suffering is relieved or they feel better they describe themselves as being "young and vital."

Developmentally, children who from an early age have abnormal features may have a body image that is significantly

disordered. Unfortunately psychiatric thinking on this issue
has been inconsistent over the years. Whereas early psychiatric writing indicated it was obvious that physical deformity
could lead to psychopathology, beginning with Freud, and for
some time thereafter, psychiatrists looked for inner
psychologic conflicts when a patient failed to adapt to outer
physical features, especially if such features fell within the
normal range. Now, however, it is apparent that the issue is
more complex (Kalick 1982). For example, studies of children
with craniofacial defects reveal an underlying association of
physical attractiveness with goodness, and ugliness with badness. Parents take less pride in children with defects, and the
birth of a child with a defect requires appropriate parental
grief and adaptation. Studies of the psychological consequences of cosmetic surgery on deformed children repeatedly
demonstrate a positive change in overall interpersonal behavior, from withdrawn to more confident and outgoing (Belfer
et al. 1982). Therefore, a positive improvement of the body
image, through either cosmetic surgery or other treatments
to ameliorate disease or eliminate "bad parts," may lead to
an improvement in the total sense of the bodily self, even to
the extent that there is the desire to exhibit the changes in
the body. However, for most patients who have been afflicted
with illness and who have recovered, there often remains a
feeling of vulnerability; and if there are residual physical or
mental defects, a sense of having been seriously injured
(Orbach and Tallent 1963).

    If a child perceives himself or herself to be defective emo-
tionally or psychologically, he or she invariably has increased
feelings of shame and a poor body image even if he or she is
considered by others to be strong or beautiful. Despite the
general wisdom that beauty is only skin deep and that beauty
is in the eye of the beholder, attractive children are preferred
by parents, teachers, and peers, and are universally rated to
possess positive features of every kind, including insight,
kindness, and intelligence. It is not surprising, therefore, that
attractive children, adolescents, and adults so treated in turn

feel more confident and capable, are more socially outgoing, and achieve greater success both socially and intellectually. Disfigured or unattractive children are much more likely to be considered unintelligent, uncooperative, unfriendly, and to be treated harshly (Pertschuk and Whitaker 1982). However, although individuals with deformities are initially perceived negatively, afterwards they may be regarded more sympathetically by acquaintances (Nordlicht 1979).

Physical attractiveness, thus, invariably leads to a response from the external world that has a significant impact on an individual's developing self-image. Consequently, individuals who request cosmetic surgery are more likely to be found on psychological testing to be anxious or neurotic, and manifest other psychosocial behaviors consistent with poor self-image. On the other hand, cosmetic surgery often increases the self-value of such individuals by helping them to feel attractive. Nevertheless "the more unrealistic the patient's expectations are with regards to the change in physical appearance, the stronger the possibility that he or she will develop adverse emotional reactions to any form of illness that effects a change in the body image" (Baudry and Wiener 1975, p. 129).

OBJECT RELATIONS EFFECT ON
BODY IMAGE IN LOSS

Grief is the normal reaction to loss, with its well-known characteristics of shock and denial, anxiety, anger, pain, despair, and disorganization. According to Bowlby (1961), grief and mourning involve three stages: in the first, there is persistent attention directed to the lost object, with feelings of intense yearning, anxiety, anger, and intense pain. In the second stage, with the recognition that the object is inevitably lost, there is numbing disorganization and despair. In the last stage, there is reorganization and replacement of the lost object with new ones. According to Engel (1961), grief is "natural and normal in the sense that a wound or burn are natural or normal responses to physical trauma" (p. 19). According to Tarachow, analysis in the usual sense must always be interrupted to accommodate it because no other work can be at the time of loss except mourning (Tarachow 1963). Freud compared mourning to bodily injury and felt that the pain of mourning was for the purpose of allowing the aggrieved to let go (Freud 1917). In classic psychoanalytic writing, emphasis was placed on identification with the lost object as the main process involved in mourning. The identification process was regarded as a means for compensating for the loss that was sustained, and it involved instinctual desires, regression to primary narcissism, and unconscious conflicts. The basis for this assertion was from simple observations of individuals in mourning and the frequent occurrence of guilty self-reproach with its self-directed aggression.

Bowlby, on the other hand, related grief to the infant's tie to its mother, the rupture of which leads to separation anxiety, mourning, and the development of pathological character states. He drew on ethnological studies for evidence of his underlying assertions with regard to separation anxiety (Bowlby 1961).

Modern object relations theory, however, being somewhat differently organized—with the sense of self constructed from the synthesis of the internalized self–object representations— has different implications for the nature of grief and mourning. The intense yearning for the object which is lost can be understood to be as much an effort to sustain the former self (for in the loss of the object it is as if the self is also lost) of the sustaining self–object unity.

Just as object loss can precipitate grief, so can loss of a part of the self through illness or injury cause separation anxiety and other pathological affective states. Because of the close juxtaposition of internal self and object representations, loss of any kind is most often represented either by physical symptoms and bodily complaints, or by clinging interpersonal behavior. Similarly, anger at the lost object can be experienced as *self*-directed for the same reasons. Because of this anger, anxiety may intensify for fear of retribution from the remaining self–object.

The disorganization and despair characteristic of the second phase of mourning occur because of the dissolution of the former self–object constancy. Object constancy, and the sense of self that is continuous, is a highly symbolic organization and a synthetic creation of the mind. Although we think of it as an inner image of the self which is distinct and fixed, it is relative and fluid. Object loss will resonate with all other significant representations of the same symbolic object to severely disrupt the sense of an organized and truly constant self. As a result, certain losses can lead to regression and an explosion of painful affects that may be as intense as acute physical trauma.

The most severe disorganization that we know of in response to loss occurs in young children who are in the process of separating and attempting to develop a sense of autonomy while differentiating from the mother who is at the same time the object upon whom they are completely dependent. In adolescents or adults with severe character disorders, disorganization also occurs at times of loss, and is commonly associated with protracted pathological mourning. Mature adults, on the other hand, are the most differentiated and therefore least likely to undergo extended or intense disorganization.

In the final stage of mourning, adaptation and a reversal of regression occur, through a psychic reorganization and a creative process of replacement of the lost object with new objects and a new sense of one's self. Vaillant emphasized that those who do resolve loss do so because of the ability to internalize, and that they do so because of prior successful separation and individuation that have been enabled by love (Vaillant 1985).

The new self that is gradually crafted through imagination and verbalization is flexible, and with the passage of time, internalized. According to Pollock (1978), creativity is a fundamental quality required for resolving the mourning process. It is in this manner that the self is reshaped, remolded, and reintegrated. The resolution of grief from loss or illness comes about through an active psychological process. Recrafting the self image through the replacement of lost objects with new objects intensifies the developmental process at any stage of the life cycle in which it occurs and amplifies that stage in the individual. This change is either for the good, with an enhanced sense of inner depth or strength, or for bad, with an ongoing sense of neediness and vulnerability.

With regard specifically to the medically ill, not only are grief and mourning like an open wound, but physical injury or change in the body image through disease or trauma also leads to an identical grief and mourning response and the search for safe and securing objects. In the same way that object loss can precipitate grief, so can part-self loss through physical injury or disease cause interpersonal separation anxiety. Furthermore, because of the juxtaposition of self and objects, anxiety about object loss is most often manifested by physical symptoms and bodily complaints.

VERBALIZATION AND SPEECH IN BODY IMAGE

Although in psychotherapy speech and the ability to communicate are taken for granted, they are essential physical attributes of the body image that at times may also be affected and thus have implications for object relations. The ability to speak evolves over time in the child with increasing control over the sphincter-like activity of the combined larynx, pharynx, and mouth. Like the control of other excretions, the production of speech regulates the control of physiologic states of tension by exteriorizing an inner space to the outer environment (Hagglund and Heiki 1980). The inability to adequately regulate speech leads to urgency, increase in tension, and frustration. Speech is also the most rapid and subtle means of communication, and is especially important in helping to maintain psychological equilibrium during periods of acute stress. Verbalization facilitates the adaptation to loss through the expansion of inner thoughts and feelings. It is the ability to verbalize that promotes the creative process.

It is not surprising, therefore, that this confirms the pattern observed by Katan in developing children that "Verbalization of perceptions of the outer world precedes verbalization of feelings" and "when we succeeded in helping these children to verbalize what they felt instead of acting upon it, we found that they demonstrated a mastery over their feelings and this mastery led secondarily to a feeling of greater security" (Katan 1961, pp. 186–187). Furthermore, it has been noted that adolescents or adults who have a poor sense of personal identity and body image verbalize poorly (Hayman 1965) and that individuals with immature personalities act out in therapy and tend to express themselves nonverbally, as do those with somatoform disorders (Edgecombe 1984). Medically ill patients who are unable to verbalize adequately also commonly act out when they become frustrated, including behaving in an overtly destructive manner. According to Stoudemire (1991), somatic verbalization of affect (somatothymia) is not only the norm worldwide, but is also especially true in psychosomatic illnesses. However, because verbalization of feelings and affect begins first with somatic representations and only later is extended to highly symbolic abstract words, during periods of stress or illness patients who are regressed and unable to articulate well may condense their expression of complex feelings into narrow somatic and interpersonal expressions such as: "I'm in pain," or "It hurts."

It is thus ironic that in a number of illnesses such as stroke, or where patients are on respirators, and at a time when they are subjected to the highest possible combination of acute stressors, patients concurrently suffer a major interruption in their ability to verbalize, and so are unable to more closely relate to objects to lessen their tension. The limited verbalization that occurs in these conditions follows a specific pattern. Because speech is limited in quantity, it tends to focus primarily on immediate issues such as physical needs and discomforts, with the expression of inner feelings and fears being quite limited.

Under such conditions, some individuals who can not verbalize complex feelings can hardly express themselves at all.

According to Greenson, "Between silence and speech lies the important realm of sounds. Great emotions are wordless but not soundless. Panic, rage, grief, and ecstasy are expressed not in speech but in sounds" (Greenson 1961, p. 80). These powerful emotions lead to involuntary cries, gasps, or laughs occurring at moments when a person is being overwhelmed by feelings or in desperate need. Analysts must therefore be especially alert in these individuals for nonverbal expressions of inner emotions in facial expression, body postures, and emotional sounds that emerge in otherwise silent lapses. The ability of patients to integrate overwhelming feelings into a new and more fluid identity and body image may be related to the degree to which they are able to communicate their worst fantasies and fears to an analyst who is skilled in responding to these nonverbal expressions (Antonoff and Spilka 1984).

BODY IMAGE AND THE SELF

It is clear that the older concept of body image as it was elaborated includes almost everything that we today would call "self" in object relations terms. The concept of body image may have been lost, or at the very least misplaced, because it is too easily confused with physical appearance, and so may have been regarded as far too superficial to be taken seriously by analysts.

But in many ways the older concept of body image has reemerged as self. As we all know, object relations are always bilateral, with the inclusion of both the self and object. If a self does not exist without relationship to objects, then we may conclude that body image also, as the core self, only exists in relationship to objects.

Suffering not only leads to changes in our body image, either physical or psychological, but also to changes in our relations to objects. The object relations so exposed, or acted out during periods of illness, can be primitive and conflicted—usually in regard to behaviors around dependency and trust. Conversely, loss of objects leads to changes in the self and body image that are manifested by physical symptoms and somatization.

Furthermore, as noted above, so many individuals, and certainly most of our patients—and sometimes even ourselves even if we are not religious—have powerful resurgent feelings of religious faith at times of profound loss, including participation in religious rituals. At times of loss and feeling shattered, faith as a state of self-cohesion and transcendence promotes a feeling of being whole again (although reconfigured). In other words, faith serves as a means to maintain the continuation of the object—as it softens the pain of the loss and allows the gradual mastery of the change and a recrafting of a new sense of self. Melancholia, on the other hand, is the sense of hopelessness and helplessness and disorganization experienced with the collapse of faith and the inner sense of bitter and irredeemable isolation and abandonment.

Because of the presence of loss and the regression to earlier states that illness induces, patients are likely to resort to splitting and to idealize the ones in whom they have faith or devalue others whom they reject. Consequently, one of the most challenging kinds of therapy is working with patients with chronic illness who are noncompliant. Because of the difficulties they present and the intense countertransference reactions they elicit, they are often referred to as the "hateful patient" (Groves 1978). It is readily apparent that these are individuals with pathological grief reactions who have failed to adequately adjust to or integrate the changes in their body image as a result of an illness or chronic disease. Instead of resolving their grief and accepting their new self, they remain regressed, helpless, despairing, and angry. They project their anger and resentment onto others and then pressure them to accept the projections (Goldstein 1991). These patients insist that all others submit to a rigid and unconditional acceptance of the righteousness of their suffering and of their entitlement to complete disregard of the needs and limits of others. They then identify with and internalize the hostile rejections that they illicit in the others and withdraw into self-pitying victimization and noncompliance.

No matter how they are manifested, hurt and anger directed at internal object relations will be played out in therapy and will require both the observational skills of the analyst to help the patient to verbalize his or her grief, and empathic participation by the analyst to help secure the patient and soothe his or her excessive internal tension states while biological treatments take their time to have an effect.

In making an analogy between the newer concept of self and the older concept of body image, the only attribute that attaches itself more readily to the former than to the latter is the capacity for self-reflection and self-observation—or what might be called the transcendent self. What becomes of the observing self with progression through the life cycle?

As we all know, life is filled with loss and our body image changes both gradually and precipitously along the way. In time we suffer the loss of youth and vitality, we lose our hair or our menstruation or ability to have babies, and even our ability to make love. We lose loved ones, and even excessive prideful love for ourselves. We lose the ability to concentrate and remember, and we lose our vision, hearing, or teeth. If we survive, and live long enough, we observe ourselves to have lost most of whatever we took for granted. In general, there are two possible ways to deal with all these losses: we either mobilize defenses, which leads to pathological grief with persistent rigidity, anger, or phobic avoidance; or we "transcend" through faith and accept the self as still good enough after a period of creative grief work, and forgive ourselves for not being who or what we once were.

Case History

As we mentioned above, psychoanalysts themselves may not be more adept at their transitions than anyone else. M. was a 75-year-old psychoanalyst with Parkinson's disease who presented with the symptoms of depression. In addition to poor sleep and concentration he felt that he was a phony who had wasted over forty years as a psychoanalyst, and who had probably mistreated his patients and misguided the many students he had supervised over the years. He specifically came to me because he did not want psychotherapy and wanted instead to be treated with antidepressants.

Because he was symptomatic and met the criteria for major depression, he was started on a low-dose antidepressant. However, the patient did agree to enter into face-to-face supportive psychotherapy to discuss his difficulties specifically associated with Parkinson's disease. It was clear that this episode of depression was precipitated by the patient's inability to continue in practice as an analyst because of cognitive deficits associated with Parkinson's disease. He confessed that he "never imagined" that he would grow old and have to deal with declining health and capability, despite having treated many patients who had. He had an extraordinarily powerful, narcissistic investment in his intelligence, insight, and capacity for reasoning, which was compensatory for a body image that was otherwise clumsy, unattractive, and unmanly. His investment in analysis was such that he would joke that "I will probably still be analyzing myself on the way to my own funeral." He was terrified by the continuing threat of the loss of this highly cathected body image, which he associated with fears of abandonment, and which he had struggled with from an early age.

His mood brightened quickly (even though he was on subtherapeutic levels of antidepressants) as he found reason to attack my training, sought and found fault with my observations and interpretations that were not classically argued, and as he sought to write new academic papers for presentation. He wished intensely for others to admire his brilliance—especially his colleagues at analytic meetings. M. was in fact extraordinarily bright and was able to bitterly interpret his own narcissistic rage that lay behind the fantasies of outdoing his colleagues, even as he competed with me and envied me for my younger age and better health. On the other hand he despaired of ever evolving psychologically at this point after having failed in three prior psychoanalyses lasting a total of fifteen years.

After only a short time in therapy I confronted M. with the observation that because of the inevitable course of his neurological disease he would have no choice but to give up his narcissistic investment in his current body image and substitute instead trust in his interpersonal relationships, and to give up his grandiosity for an attitude of being merely "good enough." M. then almost immediately stopped taking antidepressants and continued in therapy for twelve years as he struggled with his disease and underwent massive cognitive, physical, and neurological degeneration.

M. used me as a self-self/psychological object to mirror his psychological intactness as he lost the capacity to organize and remember and became helpless and dependent. Although his body image deteriorated and almost dissolved, his sense of psychological intactness was able to transcend the gaps. His synthetic ability to analyze was the primary quality of his mental body image and its retention was the prominent work in therapy. We grieved many losses as I assumed the empathic position of experiencing his deterioration both cognitively and physically. We also laughed uproariously while recounting the hopeless and failed efforts made to avert the stumbling and bumbling about in social situations that were an inevitable part of his day-to-day life.

The fantasy of an omnipotent mind that somehow endures forever, fundamentally unchanged, or that observes in a detached but intact state to the very end is grandiose, or at the very least naive! With the progression of physical illness, even the observing ego weakens before flickering out. And with it is ultimately lost the ability to maintain the securing, transcendent observing self. The self that is able to say, in effect,

"I am still here" no longer is! And with the loss of the observing ego, the psychological self dissolves and functionally returns to the equivalent of itself before separation-individuation. We become reactive and unable to manage our internal states of tension. We become dependent on the ministrations of those who care for us, comfort us, feed us, and who physically touch us. With the progression of physical illness to the end, we lose the differentiation of self from object.

SUMMARY

Body image is intimately connected to fundamentals of object relations theory. There can be no body image without a complex internal play of associations. Those with an especially shameful body image often have a poor sense of their selves that transcends the reality of their physical appearance (this will be discussed below).

With regard to suffering, even before the actual initiation of biological treatment of dysregulated disease states, healing begins through interactions with important objects. It is apparent that empathic participation by the therapist can promote healing, and that the good listener is the best physician for those who are ill in mind or body. Empathic participation in psychodynamic psychotherapy enhances verbalization. By doing so it facilitates the process of integrating the new body image and personal identity throughout the life cycle. Psychotherapy is also a creative and dynamic process that is unique to each particular doctor–patient encounter; the more it is individually crafted, the more likely it is to be successful in aiding the patient in resolving grief and the mourning process. Through the resolution of grief it helps to recreate anew the transcendent securing self.

For these reasons, the role of the therapist with patients with poor body images is an expanded and active one where one must be able to empathize with the patient's suffering, yet remain sufficiently detached so as to be able to identify with other efforts to help them with their illness. The therapist must skillfully interact in difficult circumstances with patients who somatize and who are unable to verbalize adequately. All too often, however, some analysts seek to participate in a verbal interchange and psychotherapy of highly abstract meaning. For those therapists, work with patients who have defective body images and who verbalize poorly can, therefore, be quite frustrating. The therapist must be alert to and strenuously resist the patient's efforts at projective identification, which, as in therapy with patients with significant character disorder, often lead to therapeutic impasse.

Because of the identifications with one's patient, the analyst may encounter intense countertransference reactions that directly affect the substance of psychotherapy and which may lead the analyst to withdraw from patients with severe or chronic illness. The analyst who is informed about the role of object relations in body image is always on the lookout for object loss and grief and prepared to inquire about it. At other times, with patients who verbalize poorly, the therapist may have to express for the patient who is severely regressed what they are unable to express themselves, which requires actively imagining what it is like to be in the patient's position (and which in some circumstances can be most unpleasant).

Ultimately however, psychodynamic psychotherapy reaches its limits. With the loss of the observing ego and the transcendent self, individuals again become dependent, helpless, and unaware of themselves and their body; they end the life cycle as they began it. The cycle then comes full circle, psychologically speaking, which is the way it should be.

4

Shame

Pride goeth before destruction and a haughty spirit before a fall.

—*Proverbs* 14:18

SHAME AS A CROSSWALK

In the previous chapters we developed at length the foundation that object relations establishes for the important psychological states of faith and body image. With regard to faith, we delineated its development as a natural outcome of the trust in the empathic self–object relationship between the child and its primary objects. Body image, as a fundamental precursor of the self, was also tied to the self–object relationship from early development. The ego, as Freud stated, "is first and foremost a bodily ego" (1923, p. 26). The differentiation of a healthy psychological self from the body self occurs in response to empathic parenting, in concert with the progress the child makes in separation and individuation and the internalization of cohesive self–object representations. Conversely, pathological object relations arising early in development lead to an undifferentiated and negative body image, deficits in trust and faith, and a variety of symptoms and character pathologies.

However, besides making assertions that these internal states do occur as outlined, is there any clinical evidence that supports the relationship between object relations, body image, and faith? Is there another way to join faith and body image, and if so, to what advantage?

In this chapter we hope to demonstrate that shame is a natural bridge between faith and body image on one hand and object relations on the other. Shame is a real-world event that is subjectively experienced and objectively observed in therapy. It is intimately associated with psychopathology and a common source of enormous pain reported by our patients. Not infrequently, it is the primary disturbance, the major reason for continuing in therapy, and the major focus of the analytic process. As an affect, shame exists apart from anxiety, depression, anger, or pain, although it does frequently commingle with them. Shame applies to feelings related to the body image but also simultaneously applies profoundly to feelings regarding the psychological self.

Shame is a distinct and important affect that is experienced as embarrassment, humiliation, shyness, inadequacy, and inferiority. Some children are observed to be constitutionally more shame-prone from a very early age and subsequently tend to be more rejection-sensitive in social situations, and to suffer separation anxiety. Undoubtedly, therefore, neurobiological mechanisms play a significant role in some patients who suffer from pathological shame states, and pharmacologic agents may someday alleviate the suffering of these individuals as anxiolytics, antidepressants, antipsychotics, and analgesics have aided so many others. Cognitive and interpersonal therapies—otherwise known as assertiveness training—are the most common approach for patients with severe defects in shame sensitivity and social phobia, and have resulted in moderate success overall. The underlying belief is that shame is a state resulting from failures of self, habitually learned, induced by repeated practice, and also socially reinforced, especially in women. However, despite its frequency and severity, shame is perhaps the least understood affect, and is often highly resistant to therapy. An examination of shame should therefore have implications for faith and body image, and conversely, those concepts should shed light on our understanding of shame and the approach to it in treatment.

For the most part shame has not been seriously differentiated from guilt by psychoanalytic writers in the past. In fact the words have been used interchangeably except with respect to context. Shame is often used to describe the affect subjectively experienced by patients in response to their psychological circumstances. Guilt more typically is the term used to discuss the intrapsychic mechanisms as objectively interpreted by the analyst. Shame's distinct difference from guilt has only been recognized recently. Whereas guilt implies a recognition of actions and wrongdoing for which one may judge that one deserves punishment, shame is associated with a painful feeling that something with regard to the self is wrong, undesirable, or "bad." A person shamed feels unloved by others, or even unlovable by themselves (Wallach 1994).

Shame and not guilt may be the affect primarily associated with characterological depression. The wish for revenge may be associated with a wish for humiliation, vicariously experienced (Lewis 1987). In common parlance when we talk about shame we recognize statements such as: "You should be ashamed of yourself" or "You should be ashamed to be seen like that." The first usage implies that the person is bad for something he or she is or something he or she has done or said. The second usage implies some badness related to one's appearance or physical state. Guilt is far more limited to feelings about specific acts or behaviors.

Humiliation and rage are an essential component in shame states, and laughter is a primary means to discharge shame from the self. (Guilt cannot readily be discharged by laughter; guilt requires penance.) Triumphant laughter can discharge both shame and rage by the humiliation of another (Retzinger 1987), and shared laughter can bind groups tightly together through the humiliation and exclusion of outsiders.

OBJECT RELATIONS AND SHAME

The experience of shame in common parlance requires two objects: the observer and the observed. Shame, like autonomy (its polar opposite [Erikson 1950]), always involves a mirroring object, one that can reflect both the body image and/or the psychological self.

Most children, of course, do not start off life ashamed. At a very early age, while making strides in separation and individuation under the care of a nurturing parent, most children learn to take pride in their bodies and their abilities. Children are, most often, carefree if not exhibitionistic at this time and may be summarized as described by Anthony (1981): "I am naked. I enjoy my nakedness. Everyone else enjoys my nakedness. I feel no shame" (p. 211). This state of grace is transient, however, because the child soon learns that even if it is acceptable to be naked before other children, the joy from adults is no longer readily available. In the next stage in the maturing child, even if there is no shame experienced with its own nakedness, the child learns to be ashamed when observed naked or while observing others. Finally, in the full-grown child or adult, shame may be partially felt, or even intensely experienced with one's own nakedness while undressing. This may be associated with unconscious fantasies and fears of being watched and condemned for one's shamelessness.

Girls (and later women) are more shame prone than the opposite sex for several overlapping reasons:

1. Girls are taught from an early age not to be seen and to cover their nakedness, or that their nakedness is bad or wicked.
2. Girls are also taught that their self worth is more closely connected to their body image as compared to an ideal of beauty; a failure to measure up to the ideal is mercilessly judged or experienced as failure and shame. Later, when older, women are again often judged (especially by other women) for worthiness by their ability to conceive and produce the fruits of their body, that is, children.

3. Girls are also taught never to fight or to manifest physical aggressiveness, even if wronged. Aggressive behavior in girls is actively controlled by threats of separation and verbal humiliation.

Boys are also taught not to fight and not to exhibit themselves, but these social injunctions are far less severely reinforced, and with much less verbal humiliation. Furthermore, these injunctions are inculcated at later phases in development when the boy has made a more substantial separation from the mother (who is of the opposite sex) and has turned to transitional objects or sources of masculine identification for reassurance. The older, more individuated, and by that point more verbal, active boy is, therefore, less threatened by humiliation from the mother. Finally, boys (and later men) are more commonly valued for their capability in the external world, which is more malleable than physical appearance and thus further distant from the core self and body image.

To summarize, girls are controlled by the affect of shame at an earlier age, told to cover their nakedness at an earlier age because it is "bad," and judged against the ideal according to their physical appearance and later their physical function, all of which are related to their core self body image.

From an object relations standpoint, shame in the child is related to accusation and rejection by the primary object. The object communicates to the child that the self is undesirable. The child, fearing further humiliation, withdraws and hides while anxiously awaiting the return of the object, as did Adam in the Garden of Eden. How the powerful object then behaves is critical. If the object withdraws or searches out the child for further punishment, then shame is inculcated. If, however, like God in the Garden of Eden, the child (Adam) is sought out with a receptive "Where art thou?," then the hurt is relieved and replaced by an intimacy that is once again restored.

For children who are shame sensitive, the reflection they see in the mirror of the parental object is one that is loath-

some and disgusting. Instead of a proud sense of their body
or appearance they feel weak, ugly, and undesirable. The
sense of their defectiveness extends inward to their entire
being, including internal physical functions as well as their
thoughts and fantasies. It may be projected onto any specific
physical, mental, or interpersonal attribute. They feel disgusting and unlovable.

The parental object who mirrors shame and a low sense
of self-esteem could be intrusive or seductive, or aloof and rejecting. Clearly such parental objects would be relatively
unempathic and untrustworthy. In the absence of faith in the
parental object, the child would be likely to turn inward and
find the self shamefully at fault. Conversely, an internal self-
representation associated with shame is likely to project such
feelings outward onto the surface of the body image, leading
to a defective body image, with self-doubt and anxiety about
physical attributes and abilities at various stages of childhood
development.

If the humiliating pain of the child's predicament erupts
in rage, the child learns that even its anger may be further
cause for shame because it may be met with threatened
retaliation, abandonment, indifference, or further humiliation.
The triangle of shame, lack of faith, and poor body image is
joined and internalized with pathologically disturbed internal object relations. The threat of loss is central to these relationships.

As described earlier, the normal response to loss of any
kind is grief. In grief, the symptoms that occur most commonly, second only to the affect of sadness, are physical complaints of weakness and fatigue. Chronic loss or unresolved
grief is not only associated with negative emotional affects
but also with physical distress which is internalized. This
leads to a sense of feeling emotionally and physically weak
and inadequate, with a negative body image.

It is also well known that loss in children, especially of primary parental objects or their love, is associated with fantasies of self-blame and of unworthiness. Children blame them-

selves for the loss of love and conclude that it is their own fault that they are "bad," unworthy and unlovable. These feelings of sadness and depression are generally associated with shame. Threats of loss of love, abuse, or emotional abandonment are associated with low self-esteem and poor body image, which are intimately linked to depression through shame. Suicidal impulses in depressed states, therefore, represent fantasies of revenge against the shaming "bad" self-object.

The internal object relationship can be experienced as shame with regard to one's mental self, leading to chronic depression; shame with regard to one's body, leading to feelings of inferiority or hypochondriasis; or a combination of the two. In either case, shame is the primary affect joining mind and body to the internalized object, and it occurs in response to unresolved loss incompletely grieved or mastered.

Conversely, those who have mastered losses at early stages of development, and have recrafted their self-image in a healthy fashion, develop pride and faith in their abilities, both mental and physical. Pride is the result of successful mastery of threats of loss, which in object relations terms has been enabled by empathic love.

A classic example of shame disturbance occurs in patients with anorexia nervosa. There is an intense focus on minimal changes in the body image, with many references to being fat and disgusting. There is rigid control not only of oral intake but equally as much preoccupation with control of evacuations of loathsome internal contents and products to the outer world. These patients have little faith in and are unwilling to cede control to outsiders, and their self-esteem depends on conforming to an intensely rigid set of ideal states of appearance and behavior. Deviations from the ideal are associated with intense shame that is so painful as to drive these individuals to extreme behaviors, including starvation. Because of their exquisite sensitivity to shame they are scrupulously careful in arranging the superficial conditions in interpersonal relations so that they can always claim for themselves the

position of victim in order not to have admit to any wrongdoing or aggression in their own behavior. Alas, they are rejected by peers and others for the most part because they are
experienced as too controlling and inflexible, thus continuing
the cycle of shame and distrust.

The inverse of shame is *shamelessness*. Individuals who are
flamboyant, brazen, and shameless share many of the same
psychological features as the ashamed. Their exhibitionistic
behavior, which seems to lack a situationally appropriate
sense of propriety, masks feelings of inferiority and rejection.
These characters also have distorted body images and lack
faith. It is well known that individuals abused physically or
sexually as children either grow into adults who are fearful
and inhibited, or conversely, promiscuous or aggressive. Individuals with unempathic, rejecting, or excitatory object relations may develop into adults who appear to be shameless.
They may be inappropriately seductive or provocative. The
absence of shame is therefore a warning signal of a deeper
disturbance in object relations and body image.

Case History

S., a 25-year-old high-fashion model, was hospitalized after a nonsuicidal overdose of fiorinal with codeine, a migraine medication containing barbiturate, aspirin, caffeine,
and codeine. Although her prescription was for only four
capsules per day, S. had been taking as many as thirty-
two capsules per day. S. obtained prescriptions for large
quantities of pills by rotating among six different physicians and using the opportunity of the physical exam to
sexily disrobe for them and subtlety seduce them to help
her with her migraines and fashion career. One physician,
a mere house officer in a hospital, would fill prescriptions
in his wife's name, and bring them to S.'s apartment where
he would examine her in bed.

Although S. was a success as a model—she earned up
to $10,000 a day for photographic shoots—her interests
turned to film. Despite little acting ability, and despite the

risk to her modeling career, her desire for the exposure of film was such that she actively pursued roles that were mainly pornographic.

S.'s past history was significant in the fact that she was conceived out of wedlock and was the product of a teenage pregnancy in a prominent family in a small town. S.'s mother was made an outcast and shamed not only because of the pregnancy but also because of the mother's addiction to drugs. S. was raised in poverty and was frequently forced to move around with her mother; she spent months living out of a car in a trailer park. The mother, a drug addict, would let male friends grope and comment on S.'s body. As a girl, S. was shy and easily ashamed but became tough and shameless when, as an adolescent, she surrounded herself with a gang she led by virtue of her height, beauty, intelligence, and arrogance.

The shamelessness of this patient was a hardened aggressive shell created to protect a very frightened, immature child who suffered from panic and hypochondriasis, and who was also frightened by the threats of abandonment by an immature, drug-addicted mother. Despite her physical beauty, the image she quickly projected was of ugly hatred.

S. agreed to therapy to help her keep her drug addiction from getting out of control, but refused to give up fiorinal because of her migraines. Although dissatisfied with the treatment plan, I agreed to enter into therapy to help restrict the amount of drug use but, more importantly, to keep her out of the naive hands of my professional colleagues. In therapy the patient was histrionic, needy, childlike, and demanding. She was tough, belligerent, and ugly.

S. became more trusting after I rebuffed several obvious ploys at seduction. She was motivated to be good, she wanted to please, and she wanted to be trusting. S. tapered off fiorinal and felt much healthier and in better control, and she broke off connection with the other physicians from whom she obtained drugs.

Unfortunately, the one force in her life she could not resist was her mother, who would assume a maudlin helpless tone when the patient was doing well and then influence S. to return to her through drugs. S.'s mother was
antagonistic to S. being in treatment for fear of losing her.
After nine months, therapy came to an abrupt end when
the mother came to live with her daughter and brought
with her several hundred tablets of fiorinal. Instead of love,
this patient who was shameless was weaned on her
mother's poison, and she had to remain attached if she
were to keep her mother.

S. returned unexpectedly for a consultation two years
later. She had moved cross country, but her mother was
still living with her. She had been keeping her drug abuse
under a semblance of control, but was seeing a psychiatrist who was her supplier and who had a fashionable
practice catering to the Hollywood "stars." S. had little
trust for him and was convinced he was soon going to make
a sexual pass at her. He frequently made lewd remarks to
her and referred to her vagina as a "Twinkie." S. knew she
would have to escape from him and wanted me to know
how much she missed being in therapy with someone she
could trust. To my real surprise the session ended without S. once asking me for a prescription for drugs. She had
in fact come in for a consultation for all the right reasons:
to be seen, to be heard, and to be respected.

Shamelessness is also universally recognized in narcissism.
Narcissists are brazenly self-directed and self-loving. When
it comes to personal attention, position, adoration, or material possession, enough is never enough. Narcissists are at
their cores ashamed to admit that what they really need are
other people, and in fact use a considerable amount of denial
in keeping this wish from consciousness. They may function
quite well for extended periods of time, but only as long as
they do not have to actually depend on others. Their faith in
others is quite limited and conditional, and at the very first

disappointment, even if it is minor, they will flee from the relationship. Even their own desire to love another is a source of shame.

For reasons of exposition and clarity we have been describing individuals with severe narcissistic and even borderline character pathology. They have poor self-esteem, poor body image, little faith, general affective lability, and chaotic interpersonal relationships. These are individuals for whom it is generally recognized that psychoanalytic technique must be modified to facilitate the play of projective identifications. However, there is also a place for understanding the influence of object relations on the development of body image and faith in more highly developed individuals, where shame appears from lacunae in neurotically organized character and is the primary source of symptoms.

Case History

P. was a 27-year-old recently married white male who worked as a book editor identifying new literary talent. He presented with fears of losing control in outbursts of rage and possibly injuring himself or others. The patient had never lost control except once when he was convicted of assault and jailed for six months. The family history was significant for his father and grandfather being alcoholics and his grandfather committing suicide. His older brother was schizotypal and did occasionally lose control. Although the patient was previously in therapy for two years and learned that his aggression was because of his anger at the loss of his mother at an early age, he in fact had little memory of his life before age 10.

The patient was extremely bright, expressive, and articulate, but otherwise completely normal. He was frustrated, with pent-up anger at his wife who insisted on visiting her family every weekend despite the fact that they were none too accepting of him. The patient presented to therapy after an argument in which his wife demanded that he control his temper. He did so after consulting with his mentor at work, an older woman of some repute.

It became apparent very quickly that the patient was neither aggressive or assaultive but in fact just the opposite—thoughtful, considerate, and fearful of reenacting his experience in the past. Although large and strong he felt weak, ashamed of his body, and distrustful of himself. After paradoxically being encouraged to assert himself and express his anger at his wife and her submission to her mother, he had a sudden and complete anamnesis for his early childhood.

P. was raised in a Catholic home. His mother was ill with leukemia from the patient's age 5 and would be away in the hospital for long periods of time. Although he loved her deeply he was lonely and frustrated by her absence and felt like he was being punished by God for being bad. His mother's disease remitted with treatment but recurred when he was 10. She died when P. was 12 years old. P. felt personally responsible for her death, believing that God was punishing him for his sins, such as making too much noise at home. The memory that he recovered was of how painfully he suffered feelings of longing for his mother and shame at his helplessness at her death. P. felt especially responsible because shortly after the mother's death, the father became an alcoholic, and P. had to regularly collect him out of bars and off the streets. In addition, his older brother began to act peculiarly and manifest his underlying psychopathology at school. Although P. steadfastly defended his brother and cared for his father, he felt deeply ashamed of himself and his family.

Because of his brilliant academic performance P. was able to escape the household and enter an Ivy League college on scholarship. As a junior member of a fraternity he was made a gatekeeper at a fraternity party. This party was crashed by an older man who was a non-student who assaulted one of P.'s fraternity brothers. Upon the man's return, P. confronted him at the door and an altercation ensued. The man was knocked unconscious and sued the college. His fraternity brothers claimed they knew nothing of the fight. A lawyer recommended by the college counseled P. to completely admit his part to the court. P. was then convicted, suspended from college, and incarcerated in jail for six months, where he spent his time reading. Upon release from jail and return to college he felt disgrace, as many now thought of him as a violent criminal. Although he cared deeply for his girlfriend of the time he broke up the relationship because of shame and depression. Only after five years did he again enter into a relationship, with a professional woman who found him to be a sensitive and loving man. They married over the intense objections of her mother, who wished for someone from a more prestigious background and family.

By the end of therapy (that was by no means long) P. had full, sustained recovery of his memory and felt confident to appropriately express his anger. He felt better about his body and no longer ashamed. P. felt more confident in his relationship with his wife and was proud of his accomplishments despite the serious obstacles he had to overcome. He no longer feared his colleagues' comments about jail or violent criminals and felt instead his mother's kind presence inside him. In short, he had restored a more advanced and flexible faith in himself.

PSYCHODYNAMIC TREATMENT OF SHAME

The current understanding and treatment of patients with severe shame states has been psychodynamically and psychiatrically limited. There is no specific psychiatric approach to shame. There are few conceptual models and fewer treatment strategies. Shame is generally assumed to be a phenomenological manifestation of some other underlying affective disorder, usually depression or anxiety. In both major and minor depressive disorders, obsessive guilty ruminations are characteristic, and are more common in women.

In some patients with severe shame, antidepressant medications are introduced for the purpose of treating associated major affective disorders; however, little scientifically is known about the biophysiology of shame. Some children are temperamentally more anxious and inhibited than others and are quick to respond aversely to social encounters. This may perhaps be related to physiological dysregulation, which makes them exquisitely sensitive. Therefore, it is conceivable that biological agents might someday offer some relief from suffering for some of the most disturbed individuals.

Classic psychoanalytic theory as discussed earlier tends to view shame as an earlier, more intense version of guilt. In the structural model of ego psychology guilt arises in response to conflicts in the expression of forbidden wishes and desires, either sexual or aggressive. For the most part, therefore, the treatment of shame states is no different from the manner in which guilt is handled, that is, by exploring the conflicts empathically within the transference through interpretation, which leads to the alleviation of symptoms by intellectual awareness. Unfortunately, shame tends to be resistant to the classical approach.

The analysis of shame as a separate and specific area was perhaps first discussed by Levin (1971) in terms of ego psychology and he concluded that "When psychoanalysis is successful, it results among other things in a progressive alleviation of shame" (p. 355). However, the sensitivity of these patients to the analytic situation itself has now also been recognized and the analyst must always work within the tolerance of the patient (Anthony 1981). To the patient, the analytic situation is a major source of shame because, among other things, the therapist is the one person upon whom the patient projects his or her own ideal, and also from whom the patient expects severe comparison and judgement. Silence, or even the most neutrally crafted interpretation, may be experienced as a shaming experience on the part of the patient who believes transferentially that the therapist "sees all."

The psychoanalytic treatment of shame involves an understanding of the following:

1. The affective coloring of shame is through its connection to object loss, the failure in the resolution of loss with the persistence of underlying feelings of hurt, and the wish for revenge through humiliation. In other words, shame is the displacement onto the self of the expression of the wish for humiliation of the object, in the internal self–object dyad.
2. Shame can be associated with either the mental or physical self, and usually both in severe character disorders.
3. Shame can be replaced with pride only when the underlying losses are reworked and a mental and physical self image is recrafted so that it is one in which, in its durability, integrity, and desirability to self and others, the patient can have faith.

The treatment of patients with unremitting shame in modern object relations psychoanalysis is different from the classic approach. Instead of a primary search for intellectual understanding, the patient is encouraged to enter into a close relationship in order to establish the conditions for projective identification and the intense reemergence of the associated shame states. The process of encouraging the patient to enter into this trusting relationship in which all the subjectively experienced defects are exposed in shame is naturally resisted by the patient. The patient is encouraged to reexperience all the shameful, anxious, and depressive affects associated within the early object relations. To continue the exposure in the dyadic relationship requires active, gentle, empathic encouragement of the patient on the part of the analyst. Awareness is less important than the participation in the relationship. As with panic anxiety, most patients prefer to flee from shame rather than face it. To confront shame therefore requires a leap of faith on the part of the patient that they will not be abandoned by the analyst and will be able to tolerate the pain of the underlying affect.

As the patient relates more deeply, the primitive object relations come into active play and are exposed on the surface of the relationship. The patient may feel that he or she is unworthy of all efforts to help him or her and certainly unworthy of being loved by the analyst, though he or she may crave it. This is most often observed in therapy by the repetitive and even desperate efforts the patient makes to get the analyst to disclose his or her personal feelings. Questions about the therapist's tastes, lifestyle, and opinions about the world at large are not merely efforts to resist painful intrapsychic material but also an effort to determine if the therapist could like or love someone like the patient. When confronted with the question "What would you really like to know about me?" in response, for example, to a question about the therapist's opinion about the patient's appearance, the inevitable hidden answer is "Do you love me?"

As the analysis proceeds and the early object relations are exposed, the patient invariably experiences the therapist as neglectful or intrusive. The patient will complain, and accuse the therapist of being degrading, or forcing the patient to submit to sadistic punishment. It is at this stage that the therapist must be most adept and flexible. Instead of backing away and returning to the more familiar (and more comfortable for the analyst) position of kindly idealized authority trying to treat an unworthy and hopeless analysand, the therapist must encourage the patient to endure as much pain and shame as possible in exchange for real closeness, and real faith. Only with this intensity of affect can the patient come to separate the intimacy and caring in the relationship with the therapist as uniquely different on many levels from the intent and meaning of the underlying primary object relation that is associated with shame.

The shame-ridden patient also pressures the therapist to accept as true the image of the patient as shameful in his or her needs, longings and dependency, bodily productions and appearance, and emotional reactions. The nature of the analytic interaction-relationship is one that leads to the revealing of the patient's hidden needs and fears, and thus it is quite common for the patient to re-experience intense shame. What must be communicated to the patient is the distinction between the shame that naturally erupts in therapy associated with internal object relations and the shame that the patient experiences as a result of distorted perceptions that the therapist is rejecting, hostile, or intrusive. In the analytic setting, the shame that is reactivated may be done deliberately but only because of the intent to learn the truth about the parent's inner experience, and to enable them to master the associated affects so as to free them from the protective walls they have built around themselves but that also imprison them.

Complaints are often voiced by patients, as to how artificial they feel the therapeutic relationship is, when in fact it is both intensely real and painful. It requires clarity of purpose on the part of the therapist to maintain continuous vigilance of the transference and countertransference, and flexibility in judgment. For the patient, the process is a continuous test of faith and courage to honestly face the truth. Most often, analytic cure in these patients is incomplete—just as no therapeutic relationship is perfectly matched. Many errors are made along the way and some pathological internal relationships remain stubbornly locked in. However, a "good-enough" relationship leads to considerable amelioration of shame for the patient as a result of modifications in the primary internal object relations. Analysis can not fully eliminate the scars of the original object relationship but it can convert them. Patients who feel dirty and shameful can come to feel proud and worthy. Through analysis dirt can be converted to soil. Instead of being used to hold the dead, the soil created in the analytic relationship can be used to nurture the living.

SUMMARY

Persons with excess shame feel excessively weak or ugly, and their body images are grossly distorted both physically and mentally. Everything about their bodies (inside or outside) or their psyche (internal or interpersonal) can be a source of great discomfort. They have little faith in themselves or others. If faith is understood as requiring transcendent unconditional love, then where there is shame there is also a lacuna of faith. Therefore, body and soul are linked together, whether in the pride of being lovable or in the shame in feeling that one is not so.

5

Technique

The imagination which disposes of the events of a poem, romance, tragedy, or comedy, and which attaches the characters and the passions to different personages; this requires the profoundest judgment and the most exquisite knowledge of the human heart; talents absolutely indispensable . . . for laying the foundation of an edifice.

—Voltaire, "Imagination," from
The Philosophical Dictionary

Now that we have discussed at length the subjects of body (body image and healing) and soul (faith), as well as the crosswalk between the two, in shame, we are now in position to discuss the implication of these theoretical constructs for psychoanalytic and psychotherapeutic technique. We will not review the entire body of psychoanalytic technique because that would be a major undertaking well beyond the purview of this book. We will, however, make comment on particular areas of standard technique upon which our propositions have special bearing. But first we will present a most extraordinary case that would challenge any practitioner from any theoretical or clinical orientation—the case of Ms. A.

THE CASE OF A.: "WHO DO YOU PREFER?"

A., a 38-year-old white female, was referred by her internist for evaluation. In addition to a long-standing history of anxiety, panic, and migraines, she had a chronic pain syndrome related to her gastric ulcer disorder. She had multiple other physical symptoms for which she had undergone multiple medical workups, including a two-week inpatient medical hospitalization, which was inconclusive.

The patient first presented herself by tripping and literally falling into our office. After recovering her composure, she offered complaints of dizziness, trembling, and nervousness, and a feeling of splitting apart into pieces, all symptoms that were of chronic duration.

She offered a past history of drug use and drug dependency, including narcotics, benzodiazepines, fiorinal, aspirin, and other migraine medications. She had undergone biofeedback, relaxation therapy, hypnosis, cognitive-behavioral therapy, and dynamic psychotherapy on four occasions (at ages 16, 21, 27, and 35); on each occasion for at least two or more years at a time. She was now just seeking a psychiatrist who was familiar with pain disorders, and chronic medical-surgical illness, and who was willing to monitor and manage her drug dependency and pain syndrome.

Although she offered complaints of anxiety and dizziness, except for the tripping incident she appeared quite calm and comfortable. She was a petite and attractive woman dressed in a tailored professional suit. Her hair was unusually long for her age, reaching straight down to her waist, and her frequent brushing of it and moving it aside, drew continuous attention to it. A. was an attorney who was expert in trusts and estates and had been living in a common-law relationship for fifteen years with her "husband," who had formerly been her college professor and who was eighteen years her senior.

On the occasion of our second meeting, appearing quite calm, A. announced that she wanted to confess all, so that there would be no misunderstanding on my part if I then elected to treat her. First, she admitted to a significant past history of drug abuse which she had to hide because, when discovered in the past, it would result in her being abruptly cut off from treatment. She also gave a history of four past inpatient drug detox hospitalizations with seven years of methadone maintenance, which helped prevent narcotic abuse but which did not help her with her pain syndrome.

Secondly, she confessed to sexually seducing several of her physicians, including at least one much older psychiatrist, and then described how she intentionally enabled him to gradually transgress the therapeutic boundary. She clearly recognized that she was self-destructive, but was only vaguely aware as to why this was so. She sincerely wanted to try to help herself and she stated that she wanted to have a decent, honest relationship with a doctor so she could be helped. She felt that she could cope with the frequent migraines and chronic abdominal pain syndrome, and control her drug use if she knew that she would not suddenly be cut off from medications and thrown into withdrawal. She agreed to have her weekly drug use closely monitored and was willing to try again to work on her problems psychologically.

It was abundantly clear that A. was seriously disturbed, with major psychopathology, and a probable borderline organization. Other diagnoses that she met criteria for included panic disorder and general anxiety disorder; atypical depression and dysthymia; psychological factors affecting physical condition and factitious disorder; pain disorder; and substance abuse disorder. She was a textbook of conditions! Her contacts with the medical profession and my colleagues only compounded her problems. We agreed to take her into treatment with an understanding of close monitoring of her drug use, and with strict limits on the maximum medication we would make available to her over a week's time to enable her to continue working. We also encouraged her to participate in a Drugs Anonymous group for professionals. In addition, we agreed to begin a dynamically oriented psychotherapy twice a week.

Although she courageously remained in treatment for another eight and a half years, until a surprising and tragic end, it was my personal countertransference reaction that protected the relationship from that second session—*fear*! Initially I was angry and disappointed with my medical and psychiatric colleagues for their unprofessional behavior with this woman in the past. The falling into the office, the long chestnut hair, and the helpless act all seemed just too obvious. But it was the patient's admission of offering "fair warning" that frightened me. "Am I up against something more powerful than I know?" "Dare I assume that I am wiser than my colleagues and that I could never commit the same mistakes and terrible violations?" I decided that I might not be, and that I must always remain on guard with Ms. A. so as not to miss something that was quite different or unusual.

I soon learned about her past, and it was strange indeed! Her mother and father were descendants of a distinguished American family who were, financially, extremely well off. She grew up in a mansion with servants and summered at her grandmother's country estate. Her parents and grandparents were of the leisure class and were never employed. They were all maintained on trusts that were originally set up by her great-grandfather who was a confidant of the President of the United States. As a child, the patient was raised in isolation from her contemporaries and spent most of her time either reading or in play with her brother who was two years her junior. She had a younger sister whom she rejected from birth, and with whom she never spoke. Her father was clearly psychotic at times, and her mother was cold, unavailable, oblivious to the needs of her daughter, and frequently responded to A.'s needs by giving her pills.

The patient entered treatment, and the initial phase of approximately nine months was smooth and efficient. Together we entered into a working relationship and developed all the fundamental psychological issues that would arise or reappear with greater intensity in the remainder of her analysis. By the second week she admitted to sexual contact with her father at age 12 and promiscuity in high school and college. She also revealed that she had been raped at age 20.

A. met her common-law husband at college where she was

an undergraduate and he was a professor and father figure. At first he promised to marry her but then reneged. On every occasion that A. would threaten to leave if he did not marry her, he would panic and promise to fulfill her demands, but then again renege. Her husband refused to have children, which was initially agreeable to A. but which she later resented terribly. On the other hand, he did everything for her, and was most happy when she was childish and helpless and made to feel like "Tinker Bell."

Within the first month of therapy she brought in dreams involving good and bad doctors that clearly reflected her ambivalence toward me and the medical profession. I also took them to reflect a projection of split internal parental objects, either gratifying her with sex and drugs, or predatory and poisonous. Furthermore, she admitted to fears of being psychotic like her father and going crazy. In addition, she felt at times that she lost touch with reality and within two months of therapy she had a clear dissociative event which I witnessed in response to my inquiry: "What else do you feel when you are in pain?" The patient stated: "She is evil; she has the memory; she causes the pain." When I inquired about what she meant, she responded with: "She didn't know." She asked me if she had a split personality and said that perhaps she would be better off dead.

A. had a morbid preoccupation with death, and although she stated that she expected to die young she seemed to have a sense of indestructibility. She also frequently reported dreams of death of herself and members of her family, usually by hanging and drowning. There was also a constant preoccupation with physical suffering, with ongoing discussion of drug use, pain and anxiety, and the failure of all treatments to alleviate her misery.

The relationship in the initial phase of therapy can be characterized by communications from A. to me of the following kinds: "I am so pretty, all the other men are attracted to me; how about you?" "I am in pain. I am suffering. Why won't you help me?" "Why won't you talk to me and tell me about yourself? Why must you be so rigid and controlling? Are you afraid?" Near the end of this period A. stated, "I don't trust anyone really, and have little faith in anybody; that's why I take drugs—I know what I'll get." Throughout the initial phase I actively encouraged A. to take a chance in trusting me. A. warned me that I would not like what I would see. Nevertheless, with all my limitations, by the end of the initial phase, A. tearfully admitted feeling close to me.

The middle phase of treatment opened with the patient stating that she always felt alone in her pain, until now. Within two weeks of that confession she entered into a chaotic period of drug and alcohol intoxication, culminating in an amnesis of childhood sexual abuse by her father at age 6. He would come to her at night, feeling her all over her body, touching her genitalia, and placing a popsicle in her vagina. This happened repeatedly throughout her childhood. With the amnesis the out-of-control drug and alcohol abuse ceased, but at the next session amnesia for the sexual abuse returned and was replaced with a hostile attitude on her part for therapy and questions as to why I should know all her faults and be permitted to humiliate and shame her with my scrutiny.

The next three years of treatment involved an elaboration of the same themes but with increasing intensity. There were periods of amnesis preceded by bouts of drug abuse, especially of alcohol. During the amnestic episodes further details of sexual abuse by the father were revealed. Not only was A. regularly abused as a child but she was told by her father that she would have to die with him before she grew up.

In one session A. announced in a dissociated state: "I am going to die this summer." Slowly after that an incident on the beach when A. was 10 years old was exposed. A. was traumatized by the sight of her father trying to drown her brother by holding him underwater. A. grabbed a piece of driftwood and clubbed her father over the head and forced him to let go of her brother. The father came out of the water bloody and then sexually assaulted A. on the beach and threatened her with death if she told anyone. The whole story only came out in pieces over many months, but the summer passed without a suicide attempt. A. had also revealed that she had made serious suicide attempts every 10 years since the beach incident and that the present summer had, in fact, been the thirtieth-year anniversary.

The relationship during this phase of treatment was far more rocky than initially. A. communicated sentiments of "I am completely alone; my life is worthless while your life is meaningful." "I am empty. I am a failure. I have no children." "I love you, but you couldn't possibly feel the same about someone like me." "I am a loathsome old woman; you just care for me because it's your job." The countertransferential response was also more complicated. I had to manage repeated bouts of drug and alcohol abuse, emergency phone calls begging for help, and alternating spells of anamnesis and amnesia, all coupled with a growing concern for A.'s physical and psychiatric health. During several crises I had to recommend hospitalization which was stubbornly resisted until her symptoms slowly abated. Maintaining equidistance from projected objects which A. pressured me to accept, both intensely loved or hated, idealized or devalued, was difficult.

The psychological conflicts in the patient were also made manifest in her relationship at home. A. became more aware of her husband's effort to control her and keep her helpless and dependent and in indirectly supporting her drug abuse. She made some efforts to assert herself at home which led to bouts of accusation and humiliation. A. was also financially dependent, and despite the abuse was afraid to leave her husband.

Shame was the affect most regularly encountered in therapy as A. was becoming more open about her past. After four years, she developed an integrated memory of her childhood, including sexual abuse from age 6 onward. She now had a conscious fear of death, instead of wishing for it as punishment, and expressed a desire to live for the first time. She also revealed that when she entered therapy she did so because, while in an emotional void and a state of withdrawal, she suffered a visual hallucination of a fog coming through the wall. Now, instead, she felt my continuous presence within her and was reassured by it.

Her father sickened at this time and as he became terminally ill he turned paranoid and psychotic. Nevertheless, the patient was able to sit by him in the hospital and offer him comfort and forgiveness. She was able to maintain her equilibrium even as her mother, who had always shunned her and who had beaten her with a tray just a year earlier, now accused her of being crazy for stating that her father was terminally ill. A.'s father died and she grieved, normally.

Because of the progression of her gastric ulcer disease, A. underwent gastrectomy which revealed "G" cell hyperplasia. Postoperatively, she developed a classic postgastrostomy syndrome, and was rendered physically disabled. Financially strapped, A. overcame her shame to initiate a lawsuit against her father's estate when she learned that he had invaded her trust by forging her signature. But A. confessed that she still needed her medications from me in order (1) to maintain a bond to me, (2) to suppress her anger, and (3) to prevent the recurrence of psychosis.

Several months later A. tearfully confessed that she felt loved by me for all my efforts, and was ready to consider giving up the drugs. She herself came to understand that pills were the one true love that filled her void. A. admitted that she had saved hundreds of prescription vials with my name on them, and she was now prepared to turn them over to me for disposal.

After six years and an enormous effort I felt that we had completed the lion's share of the analytic work. In order to foster trust, I had encouraged the patient to allow herself to be drawn into a dynamic dyadic relationship in which all fears, humiliations, and traumatic memories could be reexperienced and contained. Tremendous energy was released in the process and experienced bilaterally. Because of A.'s courage, core conflicts with split internal objects seemed to have been reinternalized with awareness and faith, leading to an enhanced sense of self-esteem in all domains. Her shame diminished as her pride increased, and hopes for termination and even cure arose. I could see a light at the end of the proverbial tunnel. We no longer had to be on guard . . . who knew that we were about to be run over!

Two unrelated events occurred at the end of the sixth year of treatment which set off a remarkable change in A. In the first, A. discovered that her brother, who was the person to whom she felt the closest in the world and who she always used as a transitional object, in fact had been one of the recipients of A.'s trust money. Secondly, as a result of A.'s efforts for greater autonomy, A. was beaten by her husband, who also tore up their apartment in a rage. Within a week of these events I received calls to my answering machine from the patient in a clearly excited state: "Daddy tried to drown J. and he is going to kill me." A. was taken by the police to the local psychiatric emergency room and released within a few hours in a completely normal state. In my office the next day A. had amnesia for the events of the night before, but, curious about the message that she left, she asked to listen to it.

As the message played, the patient's eyes started blinking rapidly, with an upward gaze, and A. appeared to enter into a dissociated state. A.'s facial appearance hardened as did her tone, which became disdainful and pitiless. She said: "She is so pathetic, isn't she? I am really going to have to kill her someday." "I am the one who makes her suffer—that coward—she gave me all the memories." "It is so good to be out again." "I've been watching you all these years." Startled, I asked, "Who am I with right now?" and the patient answered: "R." Whereupon, R. disappeared and A. returned, amnesiac.

Two weeks later A. had what appeared to be a bout of hysterical psychosis, whereupon she was admitted to the inpatient psychiatric service. However, again A. normalized within several hours with amnesia for the entire episode. This time I elected to do a full drug detoxification and her husband agreed to enter into therapy with A.; however, he was also

observed by the emergency room staff to be quite threatening to A. and physically abusive. The hospital stay was completely uncomplicated and of little benefit, for immediately
after discharge A. began abusing alcohol again, and a few
weeks later the patient came to my office and announced: "It's
me, R. Give me back the drugs or I'll leave therapy and kill
A." I inquired of R. as to how she got her name and she told
me that "It is a name she picked from a novel of a woman
who comes back to haunt the house."

Although I long pondered (and consulted with colleagues)
whether I was dealing with an individual with a primitive
psychotic core, who was delusional, I reluctantly concluded
that the patient had a stable alternate identity consistent
with multiple personality disorder, a diagnosis about which
I shared a great deal of skepticism and had never previously
encountered. I was also deeply concerned whether I had
through my countertransferential management of her projected objects induced a new split through my encouragement
of a closeness that was intolerable for A.

A. had no awareness of R. but would request that I "not
let her kill me." "I know I am bad!" This was usually followed
by: "What did I just say?" The transition from one alternate
to another had a psychotic quality and each would describe
a sense of being annihilated by the other as they entered the
transition. R.'s return was more frequent now and she would
plead with me not to abandon her. "I remember everything."
"I am the one who deserves to live." "A. is helpless and weak."
"I am the strong one."

Then suddenly at one session R. announced: "Who do you
prefer? You have to choose because you only have thirty days
to decide." I replied, "I will not abandon A. and I cannot
choose one more than the other." Immediately then A. returned with amnesia, and I repeated to A. the same message
with regard to R.: "I will not abandon R., and I cannot choose
one more than the other." A. replied: "Who is R.?" Over the
next month A. and R. played hide-and-seek with each other,
leaving alternate messages on my answering machine. R.

would call to say that she loved to torture A., and A. would call to ask me to get "her" to stop torturing her.

A. also gave a forty-year history of "blackouts" and feeling as if she had been taken over by another person. She stated that in the incident on the beach at age 10 it was someone else who clubbed her father, even though it was definitely she who was sexually molested thereafter. It was clear that there was a definite long-standing split between the long-suffering, sexually assaulted, timid A. and the retaliatory, uninhibited R. Drugs and alcohol were chronically abused by both to dull the pain of and perhaps facilitate the transition between the alternate states.

Finally, in one session, R. revealed when she came into being. When A. was 4 years old, her cat had six kittens whom she loved. Her father, however, told her that she could not keep them and took them and A. outside to the shed to drown them in a rain barrel. A. protested and cried bitterly. Her father said he would only stop drowning them if A. licked his popsicle (penis). A. refused. One by one the kittens were drowned by her father until finally, to save the last one, A. relented and licked her father's penis. It was then that R. began, and it was R. who was then crying deeply in my office. The very next session A. came in and said that she knew everything; she knew who R. was; and she felt for the first time that someone was not chasing after her to kill her.

Over the next year A. consolidated her identity and for the first time was able to view with remorse the devastation of her life that her illness had caused—mentally, physically, and socially. She also increasingly understood that her husband was a controlling, assaultive codependent who required her to be a helpless, submissive girl. As A. improved, his threats to kill her or lock her away increased. A. decided to move out instead of remaining with him, and within six months she was feeling more secure on her own and beginning to pursue a new career. After just a few months more of living on her own and working as a photographic assistant she genuinely felt happy and optimistic for her future. It was then that she suddenly, tragically and without warning, died of a heart attack.

GENERAL OVERVIEW: THERAPEUTIC STANCE

Practioners of psychoanalysis struggle to cleave to a standard, universally agreed-upon structure. However, because at its core psychoanalysis is intended as a process to achieve relief from suffering and to encourage individual well-being, standard structures are always under pressure to conform to individual needs. Besides, many understand that the epistemology of psychoanalysis lies somewhere between science and poetry—a dyadic revelation (Nadelson 1996). Nevertheless, principles, structure, and approach are agreed upon by most practioners. Variations in psychoanalytic technique, although usually attributed to differences of theoretical formulation, usually begin as a result of personal struggle in therapeutic settings. Although it is commonly believed that theory and technique develop concurrently, in actuality psychoanalytic technique pursues an inexorable development that usually receives theoretical justification only after the fact (Jackel 1966).

Despite the diversity of psychoanalytic perspectives that have been pursued worldwide, perhaps the most significant clinical debate over the past two decades has occurred between proponents of classical drive-oriented, conflict/ego-defense theory and proponents of modern, object relations and self-psychological, deficit-based theory (Aron 1990, Scharf and Scharf 1995, Tuttman 1987). This debate has resulted from a fundamental argument with regard to whether developmentally we psychologically begin as entities seeking gratification of drive states and the avoidance of pain, or whether we begin as entities, first and foremost, wired for attachment to objects and the means to maintain those attachments (Bowlby 1960). This debate also involves consideration of the theory of the development of symptoms and psychopathology as a result of part mechanisms developing into whole psychic entities, versus the effect of synthetic dyadic wholes breaking into symptomatic parts under stress. Technically, many practitioners utilize a flexible approach, simultaneously incorporating both poles of the theoretical spectrum in their analytic investigations.

Modern psychoanalysis involves an exploration of unconscious internal objects as they are projected onto the analyst within the transference, and the ways in which the patient resists those efforts to either understand or alter their distorted perceptions despite the actual experience with the analyst (Ogden 1984). Wallerstein, in his survey of international variations in psychoanalytic technique, believes the above to be the essential core of psychoanalysis (Wallerstein 1988). Our interpretations attempt to demonstrate to the patient the distortions created by the re-experiencing of their internal object relations. The resistance to change requires that the patient maintain a safe interpersonal distance while using other more primitive and inflexible mechanisms to cling to the object of the analyst. The analyst, through careful observation as well as empathic participation in the structured environment of the analytic dyad, encourages the patient to recognize and give up his or her resistance.

Classical ego psychology, although technically very sound, is also the most highly abstract. Although the patient's suffering is clearly real, the relationship, subsumed entirely within the transference, is biased to being considered the manifestation of neurotic conflicts alone; the onus for all interactions, therefore, except interpretation, is placed on the patient. So powerful was the concept of transference considered to be that Greenson (1965) felt compelled to argue for the existence of a real relationship with the analysand that was nontransferential. "Cure," which occurs in response to the analysis of the resistance and working through of the transference, is primarily considered to be due to the development of rational awareness, with the relationship being of only secondary importance. In this manner, however, the therapeutic relationship can feel unnatural, because it does not conform to any other important dynamic relationship in nature. A., for example, could never have tolerated a classical analysis. The aggression that would emerge, and the shame that would follow the attention repeatedly given to emotions and behaviors that A. regarded as loathsome would have destroyed the relationship.

Although the relationship developed in self psychology is a more natural one, with the investigation of empathic failures, it nevertheless can hold to an unrealistic expectation of the diminution of aggression and hatred in the clinical encounter in its attempts to create the goodness of an idealized mirroring object. In object-relations theory, good and bad are equally likely, given the nature of early relationships, and are easily mixed together. In other words, the developing child is neither good from the start as is implied in self psychology, or guilty and bad as implied in ego psychology. Projective identifications from both good and bad parts of the child's internal objects continuously occur within the analysis, and their bilateral experience and examination are the very substance of therapeutic change. From a technical standpoint, the analyst must be prepared to "join the battle" with the patient, who is compelled to play out all the internal objects— good and bad, loving and hateful. This struggle with the internal object relations from the past, empathically and honestly undertaken with the real patient in the present, helps to modify their urgency of expression by the addition of new layers of experience, awareness, and faith.

Therapy informed by internal object-relations theory most closely conforms to the observed interpersonal phenomena enacted within the therapeutic relationship. Technically it also suggests a vector of orientation that the therapist strives to achieve.

How much initiative the analyst will take in making transference interpretations depends on how ubiquitous he believes transference implications are in the patient's associations, how important he believes it is for these implications to become explicit, and how confident he is that they will spontaneously become explicit if he waits for them. [Gill 1982, pp. 26–27]

Taking the initiative in making transference interpretations requires an active process in constructing what Winnicott (1965) referred to as a "facilitating environment." Creating this environment, however, is a unique undertaking for each individual in therapy, and it involves an amalgam of maintaining correct boundaries, empathic participation, and respect for the patient's autonomy.

Nevertheless, in our view, to achieve the full play of the internal object relations the analyst must go further with some individuals and actively seek to draw them in tightly. As much as she sought to trust another human being, A. was suspicious of all therapists and would try to pull away from a truly intimate relationship. Although she would frequently state that: "I know I am not worthy but please help me," she regularly inserted a wall of drug abuse between us as a way to control the interpersonal relationship. My response to these efforts was to encourage her to permit herself to get closer and that our relationship potentially contained all that was necessary to help her.

A vector of orientation in psychotherapy of trying to draw the patient closer is also the most natural to interpersonal human relationships, reflecting the desire to seek intimacy. Although neurotic character structures serve to defend against true interpersonal closeness, by actively seeking intimacy with the patient while strongly defending flexible boundaries, the environment is prepared for the outpouring of the most intense thoughts, feelings, and memories upon the person of the analyst. By so doing, there is a natural reworking of internal object relations, shame, and the restoration of faith.

Modern analysis is more dynamic and more complicated than the static theoretical models of the past because therapists now are prepared to shift and adjust their stance and modes of participation and interaction in therapy in a unique mélange with each patient, and at different times within the treatment. Object-relations theory allows for a more flexible initial therapeutic alliance with patients with severe character disorder and preoedipal psychopathology than classical approaches. As the analysis progresses and the patient's internal object relations differentiate and mature, classical approaches of ego psychology can be then be utilized to enhance the efforts of a more fully integrated self.

When patients come into therapy they most often do not know what to expect. They do know that they are to talk about themselves and their troubles. Some even expect that they may be asked to lie down and free-associate about whatever comes to mind. Most do not know how the therapist is to respond, or out of anxiety may inquire to which school of theory the analyst ascribes, with little understanding of what that question involves, although nowadays (many are anti-Freudian not out of understanding of the limitations of the classical model but out of complete ignorance of psychoanalysis) they are seeking a therapist who will talk to or advise them. More profoundly perhaps, what most are seeking, but do not recognize, is the wish for someone to love and admire them.

HEALING

The Restoration of Faith and a New
Body Image (Self)

Up until now we have been discussing the stance in therapy by the analyst. But it is unlikely that psychoanalytic cure occurs either just through intellectual awareness or some passive restructuring of deficits in the internal object relations. Psychoanalysis is after all a dynamically engaged relationship that is mutually shared and bilaterally observed. It is a powerful process that directly involves us and even has profound effects upon us, and when performed well it leads to what Langs referred to as "truth therapy" (Langs 1981). It is this active seeking of meaning by the patient with the participation of the analyst that prepares the patient for change. When hidden truths are uncovered in therapy, they are initially associated with affects which can be quite intense, and which only later are followed by a sense of well being and security. These personal truths provide a foundation for a leap in faith to self–object constancy that cannot be found elsewhere in the patient's life. How or why a patient makes a leap at a particular moment in treatment is unknown. Some do so because of a coincidental alignment of external circumstances and others do so because of a fortuitous interaction within the analysis. Most would assume that the process unfolds gradually, but in fact it seems to grow in discontinuous steps and leaps.

When the patient initially comes to therapy it is usually after an experience of self or object loss. Object loss may lead to internal disorganization and regression followed by the most intense despair or anxiety. On the other hand, because of faith's effect in making one feel whole again the decision to enter into treatment itself may lead to dramatic changes in illness behavior. Anxiety and worry decline rapidly; physical symptoms and pain decrease dramatically; sleep, appetite, and activity improve significantly even before treatment takes effect on the underlying pathological state. Obviously then the most important leap of faith occurs earliest in analysis, in the acceptance of the analyst and the analytic situation, which normally involves some amount of deprivation and sacrifice on the part of the patient. This leap is especially difficult for individuals who have paranoid traits or who have been physically and/or sexually traumatized.

In the analysis of individuals with severe character disorders the central defect is assumed to be due to the lack of sufficient empathy in early development or because of neglect, excessive intrusion, or overt abuse. It is obvious therefore that empathy provided by the listening therapist can serve to restore the defect and promote healing through the restoration of faith and interpersonal connectedness. The therapy may proceed for some extended length of time however before the patient is prepared to make any further leaps. But eventually, as a result of tireless empathic effort within the analysis, heretofore repressed material or erotic feelings consciously withheld suddenly erupt within the transference and a new level of trust is obtained. At some point in virtually all analysis, hateful feelings of the most intense kind erupt within the transference that threaten the analysis itself. According to Coen (1992), "Without sufficient blood and guts coming into the analytic setting, through the patient's experiencing violence and passion in an ongoing sustained way in the analytic transference, pathological dependency can not be resolved" (p. 254). Clearly the course of A.'s therapy involved blood-and-guts revelations with intense affective shifts. Feelings of acute shame and terrible helplessness permeated the treatment. Fantasies of murderous revenge were mobilized as she struggled through the dangerous waters of psychosis. Her efforts were truly courageous acts of love and faith.

The choice for the patient between remaining stalled at the impasse of a negative therapeutic reaction (Danielian and Lister 1988) or working through the hostile transference (and not merely suppressing it) involves a true leap of faith. The object-relations informed analyst will appreciate that the borderline patient or the individual with severe character disorder, while driven by murderous desires for revenge (Chessick 1977, 1982), is simultaneously terrified by aloneness and abandonment. Flexibly making oneself available, especially after particularly painful, hostile, or shameful sessions, is necessary (Gunderson 1996). Moreover, through empathic recognition of the patient's utter despair on these occasions and the active seeking of emotional contact with the patient through, for example, taking the initiative of calling them (on select occasions) and expressing concern for them has a powerful mutative effect on the projective identifications. We have used this option on some occasions and have interrupted many a suicidal gesture.

With respect to the process of psychoanalytic healing much

clinical observation has flowed upon the underlying theory. In the drive-ego-conflict model, cure occurs as a result of interpretation of primitive conflicts projected within the transference, leading to awareness. In the developmental arrest model, psychopathology is the result of empathic failures. Although the analyst inevitably makes empathic errors, because of his or her sustained participation in the relationship in an effort to understand and promote health, the analyst becomes a new transference object that is internalized. Insight and interpretation are not necessarily primary (Glucksman 1993). However, as a result of the therapeutic process, the patient must develop an awareness that there has been a change in the body image. There will have been either a change in psychological or physical symptoms, or a change in cognitive, interpersonal, or social skills, all of which involve a change in awareness and belief with regard to one's image, either physical or psychological (both are parts of the body image). The patient by now has developed the courage to carry the burden of his or her own anxiety and deficits. This new sense of self, or body image, will have been slowly and painstakingly recrafted until it has been personalized and then internalized alongside the relationship with the analyst. A. certainly had crafted a new body image. She would no longer tolerate being considered a child and had reconfigured the relationship of her alternate identities. She was also for the first time able to see herself realistically as a middle-aged woman, and yet was for the first time at peace with her self and her age.

Ultimately, healing can occur only when the patient is prepared to let go of the transitional object of the therapist and switch to the reworked object of an independent, flexible, and relatively secure self. The transition from the middle phase of therapy to the termination phase, therefore, requires a leap of faith on the part of the patient no matter how thoroughly he or she has been analyzed up to that point, because the commitment to leave analysis is an enormous one. In the termination phase, the patient finally gives up the object of the therapist, and replaces him or her with a sustaining faith in the self. Patients may find a new pride in their body image, just as they may also come to believe that they have been faithfully loved even though that has never been actually verbalized directly to them. The shame that was attached to the body image on entering therapy will have been markedly reduced, as patients have now found the means to forgive themselves and deal with the anger attached to previous internal object relations. After all, there can be no secure faith, no resolution of abiding grief, and no recrafting of the self without the internalization of forgiveness enabled by empathic understanding.

Countertransference

To reiterate, the relational and classical analytic models lead to different ways of understanding the therapeutic process. The classical model, with its emphasis on the independence of the patient's conflicts from external objects, would necessitate the adoption of a nonintervening neutrality with respect for the patient's autonomy. The relational object relations model, with its emphasis on the importance of the external object as an agent for change, suggests the adoption of an empathic participating activity with respect for the patient's intimacy. Of note, however, is that although the classical model suggests neutrality, Freud in the conduct of his analyses revealed his wide-ranging interests and tastes to his analysands. On the other hand, although the relational object-relations model suggests a participating empathic stance, according to Guntrip (1975), he experienced Fairbairn (his analyst) as austere and detached.

Some analysts have a peaceful and receptive temperament Others like myself spill over with emotion and reaction. The temperament, however, is less important than how the analyst relates and handles the projective identifications within the dyadic relationship. Some therapists maintain a seeming impartiality which in truth is a screen behind which they hide their own fears, or fear of the patient if they were to confront the aggression of the patient's destructive, addictively enacted behavior. Too often nowadays one hears of therapists who believe that they are just innocent, caring participants, upon whom the patient's object relations just naturally come into play, but who otherwise should be recognized, and admired, if not adored, for their loving, caring attention. Patients, in their wish to be loved and gratified, will feed back to these kinds of therapists their deep love and appreciation in a ritual of mutual admiration, while suppressing all overt expressions of anger. We have treated a number of individuals who have been through several such previous therapeutic relationships. The underlying anger and sense of betrayal that eventually results in these individuals is intense. By failing to be honest about one's self and the limitations of the analytic process, the therapist introduces hypocrisy and oppressiveness into the treatment process (Slakter 1987, p. 209).

It is a pretense to think and act as if we believe that we make no considerable demands on patients. We actively enter into a relationship that is intended to draw them closer and therefore encourages the full play of their internal object relations. We expect them to reveal themselves, and subject themselves to the most painful and shameful feelings while we choose the time and the manner in which to respond to them. This is hardly easy or neutral, and it is certainly unlike any other relationship.

Some patients first develop an erotic loving transference behind which exist more secretive and threatening negative hateful feelings. On the other hand, some patients first present with aggression behind which are carefully protected loving feelings that must be sensitively elicited. The same is true with countertransference, except that by and large analysts are much more comfortable discussing their hostile reactions to their patient's demands while they carefully guard any acknowledgment of loving or erotic feelings. In all instances the analyst must continuously make active efforts to draw the patient closer, and challenge the patient's attempts to avert anxiety through the use of characterological defenses that serve to keep them safely at a distance (although with a tight grip) and their repressed impulses hidden. Only by numerous interchanges, empathically undertaken, can patients relax their defenses and allow a joining in therapy, and risk all—shame, hurt, and fear. To all the threats of "I am leaving," we must respond with "Why are you afraid of getting closer?" For those who would quickly jump into an eroticized idealizing closeness, we wait with humility for the hateful denigrating revenge. And, to all who express doubts in "Why should I trust you?" we respond "Why not me," and, "If not me, then whom, and when?"

By general consensus among analysts it is understood that clinical work is very taxing, and that carrying the burden of the patient's anxiety, pain, and hurt, while restraining one's own natural desire to withdraw, is a heavy one. For the analyst to have hostile countertransferential reactions is therefore understandable, given the analyst's effort to maintain an involved impartiality from the patient's relentless transference and dilemmas. And although understandable at times, pervasive anger and disgust are abnormal and require careful review, or additional supervision. On the other hand, loving feelings are seldom openly admitted.

The question that is seldom addressed is whether it is fundamentally necessary to love the patient in order to help him or her (Coen 1995, Slakter 1987). Solomon (1997) has recently discussed the effects associated with the analyst loving the patient. According to Frankl, "love is the only way to grasp another human being in the innermost core of his personality. No one can become fully aware of the very essence of another human being unless he loves him" (Frankl 1963, p. 176). We have previously discussed how in order to develop successive levels of faith the patient must subjectively come to trust and feel that they have been loved and well cared for within the dyadic relationship. If it is the therapist's role to empathically participate within a framework that encourages maximal individual freedom but which nevertheless is structured always to serve the well-being of the patient, and whose end is the development of a transcendent securing faith, then isn't that activity a loving one? Is not analysis at its core a nurturing, loving process? This is not to say that some erotic countertransferences that involve craving and controlling of the analysand are not strictly pathological. True love organically nurtures and grows and in analysis seeks the fulfillment and freedom and ultimate separation of the individual. Consequently, to effectively do good work, in addition to having technical competence, the therapist must be ready to nurture, and deeply care, and to do so requires that the therapist must generally be fulfilled and happy in his or her own life. Otherwise, disturbances will occur in therapy that will lead to the mismanagement of projective identifications.

REMINISCENCES: FACT OR FANTASY

The treatment of A., discussed above, raises many questions with regard to psychoanalytic technique and process, not the least of which is whether memories revealed in therapy are the authentic crystallization of facts formerly denied and displaced, or the approximate representation of impressions that have been shaped, remolded, and perhaps even distorted by an impressionable and suggestible mind. That A. had true memories of sexual abuse was undeniable. That there was an air of distortion and reworking of memories was also undeniable.

In his early cases of hysteria, Freud was similarly preoccupied, and wondered about the reliability of his patient's revelations. Initially he believed that his patients were in fact sexually abused (Breuer and Freud 1895), but, he later concluded, out of personal experience with a patient who spontaneously threw her arms around him when she awakened from a hypnotic trance, that "it had little to do with me" (Freud 1925, p. 27). (On suddenly encountering A. on the street one day, she too spontaneously approached me and threw her arms around my neck.)

It was then that Freud thought that what was ultimately more important was the belief by the patient in the reality of their experience and its subjective validity within their dynamic life narrative, rather than the certainty of verifiable facts. This of course opened the door for him to create a universal theory in the existence of sexual seduction fantasies as the cause of neurosis. But if A. did indeed suffer the most terrible sexual abuse as she described, and if, as a result, she developed a dissociative (multiple) personality disorder, as I believed she did (and not merely a hysterical psychosis), is that not prima facie evidence not only for the existence of object relations but also for the complex process of splitting? In the next chapter we will discuss in greater detail the question of truth derived in therapy.

SUMMARY

Object relations theory has had a profound impact on psychoanalytic technique by affecting the nature of the stance taken in the dyadic relationship and the management of the projective identifications. It has enabled a broader understanding of the interpersonal process as well as a more naturalistic mode to explain our relationship to the patient and the development of our own countertransference. Although object relations theory does not necessarily substitute for self psychology or ego psychology, it does underlie them, and therefore allows for a more careful consideration of the correct stance with a given individual at different times in the treatment process. As a result it more fully enables the process of reminiscence, no matter how shameful, and thus consequently a reshaping of a new sense of self—one of pride.

6

Truth

The Tao (truth) is in the Passage rather than in the Path.
It is the spirit of change—the eternal growth which re-
turns upon itself to produce new forms.
—Kazuko Okakura, *Taoism And Zenism*

In the last chapter we concluded with the question of truth
and reliability. In fact one of the most important questions
under consideration by practitioners of psychoanalysis and
psychotherapy today is the truthfulness and reliability of the
data emerging in the analytic process, given the increased
participation of the therapist within the process and the addition of his or her own subjectivity. Are the meanings derived within psychoanalysis true? The question once asked
may be broadened to include: "How reliable is the psychoanalytic process as compared to other objective and presumably
scientific modes of investigation?" "Is psychoanalysis science
or is it art, poetry, or religion?" "What also is the relationship of faith to truth?" And more broadly, "Does the theory
of object relations say anything of importance about truth in
psychoanalysis, or for that matter, anything about truth in
general?" From the outset one can reasonably expect that any
effort to attempt to address such questions is doomed to failure. Can one honestly take on the subject of truth and hope
to succeed?

Through experiencing religious faith, countless individuals (not necessarily in analysis) have found real security even in the face of extreme adversity, and peace even at times of personal loss. Religion has been used as an explanatory paradigm for events in nature for millennia. It has only been in the last century that our western culture, in the grip of scientific determinism, has swung so completely and unilaterally over to a Hellenistic rational philosophy of truth and away from the Judeo-Christian religious philosophy of truth. It is worth remembering that much of our morality and ethical sense has developed from the latter, just as technology has flowed from the former.

Object relations, because of their bilateral nature, would seem to require that truth involve duality. Can truth ever be known or must it only be contemplated? At a minimum, however, object relations do allow another interesting look at the Alice in Wonderland world of truth, and may have greater implications for it.

DUALITY AND TRUTH

Convictions with regard to truth run deeply. Subjective beliefs are held as strongly as objective opinions, and the two are often confused with each other. This polarity in thinking is not new and it stretches across the long, torturous history of philosophy. Ancient philosophers believed that God, man, and society were indivisible, and many believe that the ancients lived in greater harmony with nature then we do today (or many like to pretend so). Since those times, mankind has survived with an expanding awareness of self and has struggled to understand and explain his relationship to the world in more complex terms.

Man's initial representation of God was a personal one, and developed in parallel to his technological mastery over the world of nature. God evolved from a simple animal totem representation to a transcendent being who is simultaneously both extraneous to and immanent in "creation." Medieval western philosophers, and theologians since, have contemplated the separate natures of man and God and have tied

them together consistently only through faith. The theist's
God is a personal Being, one who is involved in man's destiny
and is immanent in creation. He is interactive with man
through miracles and commandments.

Philosophy made a great leap forward in the search for
truth with the arrival of Spinoza who emerged from his theo-
logical studies to reconceptualize existence separate from the
then prevailing notions of God in terms of what is perhaps
classic duality. In his *Ethics* (1677), he described mind and
body and physical and mental experiences as parts of *one*
process, although they might be perceived in one frame of reference as action and matter "substance," and in another frame
of reference as thoughts and mental "substance." The language applied in one frame of reference could not be applied
in the other, and while the entire world would therefore be
double in this manner, one side could not exist without the
other (Durant 1961). His vision of God was therefore a pan-
theistic one in which God represented the totality of both
polar perspectives.

Over the next 300 years philosophy reached its ascendancy
and struggled through what may be called epistemological
wars of first causes. Once God was dethroned as the direct
originator of all existence, then other intellectual theories had
to be substituted in its place. Many theories were proposed,
but generally they divided along the poles of subjec-
tive-objective experience. Beginning with Descartes (the father of modern philosophy) and his statement, "I think. Therefore I am." (which is subjectively driven), they moved through
the spectrum of Kant's *Critique of Pure Reason* (1781) to the
systematically objective theories of Hegel's (1816) *Phenomenology of Spirit* (Hundert 1989). One could view consciousness as the central organizing principle, with existence and
the entire universe being secondary to it. Or, conversely, one
could view nature and reality as systematically arranged with
consciousness being only one of its potential creations. The
philosophies of others, including Schopenhauer in *The World
as Will and Representation*, Darwin in *The Origin of Species*

(1859), and Nietzsche's (1883) "superman" with his will to power, swept through Europe in waves, all in a continuing effort to explain man's fundamental nature (Hamlyn 1987). God was now relegated to the position of indirect originator of first causes. God may have set the principles of creation but the world now continues on its own, with the further possibility of evolution, creativity, and human beings that not only act with free will, but in their relationship to the world are motivated by "reason."

The twentieth century began in a breathtaking leap of intellectual creativity in the pursuit of truth. The simultaneous discovery of Einstein's relativistic physics and quantum mechanics and Freud's unconscious mind revolutionized age-old perceptions of basic physical and mental realities. They in turn gave impetus to the early philosophical work of Wittgenstein (1922) and logical positivists, which held that all philosophical inquiry should now be restricted only to problems open to scientific investigation. Nowadays, it is the astrophysicists, artificial intelligence theorists, mathematicians, thermodynamic physical chemists, and theoretical biologists who are contemplating these same questions as they examine first causes and contemplate the possible nature of God, including the anthropic view that the world we apprehend and experience arose spontaneously out of its own infinite possibility. Everyone—from neuroscientists to philosophers—is contemplating consciousness and how felt experience is connected to the physical brain (Gorman 1997).

Meanwhile, at the opposite pole, man's search for faith and personal meaning would not be deterred, and reentered philosophy (if ever it left) as existentialism. For the antiscientific, metaphysical existentialists Heidegger, in *Being and Time* (1927), and Sartre, in *Being and Nothingness* (1943), the fundamental question was why there is anything rather than nothing (Hamlyn 1987).

Oddly enough, the philosophic father of existentialism was Kierkegaard who in opposition to Hegel's scientific approach to religious questions saw truth in a personal relationship to faith (Hamlyn 1987). Beginning as he did as a seminary student well versed in theology, Kierkegaard (1846) found the systematic theories of reasoning, even with the influence of subjective free will, quite limited and falling short of the personal experience of faith. He saw that in a world without faith and passion man feels that he does not exist. Many years later Jaspers, another existentialist, in *Truth and Symbol* (1959), viewed man as grasping at being in the subject–object polarity with an everlasting need to utilize symbols as the cyphers to a transcendental oneness. Where Kierkegaard saw man motivated by a personal need for faith, Jaspers saw the need for a transcendent oneness out of the pull of the subject–object polarity. Paul Tillich, one of the most influential theologians of our time, described religion in the following manner:

> Being religious . . . does not require a belief in the existence of Gods, or one God, and as a set of activities and institutions for the sake of relating to these beings in thought, devotion and obedience. . . . Religion in its innermost nature is more than religion in this sense; it is the state of being concerned about one's own being and being universally. [Tillich 1958, p. 29]

Victor Frankl, in *Man's Search for Meaning,* wrote of a talk he gave while in a concentration camp in dire circumstances:

> Human life under any circumstances, never ceases to have meaning, and that this infinite meaning of life includes suffering and dying. . . . the hopelessness of our struggle did not detract from its dignity and meaning. . . . Someone looks down on each of us in difficult hours—a friend, a wife, somebody alive or dead, or a God—and he would not expect us to disappoint him. [Frankl 1963, pp. 131–132]

But philosophy at the end of the millennium finds itself at a crossroads—there is no unified truth, only various systems that purport to explain experience, or to create order from chaos. And there are challenges for any system that claims special possession of truth for itself.

Science, for example, is such a system; its great strength is in knowing a great deal about very little and being able to precisely predict outcomes. Science has triumphed in the twentieth century—from aviation to space fight, from splitting the atom to deciphering the genetic code, from radio and television to robots and information processing. Science has become the new ideological God in some quarters, dressed in the costume of the true theory of everything. Science has earned its claim to truth, but for all its reasoning, verifiable facts, and magnificent technology, science rests upon assumptions that are often simplistic and assailable. Science for the most part is based on observer and subject and their relationship through measurement. It relies on deterministic beliefs in cause and effect joined by a sequential but reversible absolute flow of time. As a result, science is predictive and valid only within a very narrow range, and fails miserably to explain the behavior of complex systems (e.g., it can predict the behaviors of solids and gases but not liquids). This applies not only to complex systems, but also to microscopic ones. Determinism falls apart in the dimension of molecules and subatomic particles, where the mathematical, Schrodinger's wave function describes the many possible states of a particle—in theory. However, once a measurement is made (which is an intrusion from the macroscopic dimension) of a particle's position or momentum, only one state is found to exist; the wave form instantaneously is "collapsed." In other words, there is no symmetry between cause and effect, and one cannot predict the outcome (Coveney and Highfield 1990). Quantum mechanics exhibit a peculiar self-referential duality where a representation of measurement is also an active operator, and is therefore like the mind, in which function subsumes structure. It follows that scientific determinism as unitary truth cannot exist.

A saying attributed to Galileo is that "Mathematics is the language with which God wrote the universe." Many other theorists in science believe this to be true because mathematical abstractions, found purely by thought and reasoning, have turned out, over and over again, to provide exact descriptions of the physical world. On the other hand, the ancient mathematical abstraction *zero* upon which so much mathematical theory depends, is known not to exist. Scientists for the past half-century have known that there is no such thing as absolute nothingness. Even the vacuum of space, devoid of a single atom, seethes with subtle subatomic activity (Browne 1997). Therefore, from the standpoint of nature and reality, major mathematical abstractions are as much an illusion (and thus are as untrue) as God is to an atheist.

Where then does the sense of scientific causality begin for us apart from the experience of "suchness"? And how are we to make sense of the duality of absolute emptiness and seething fullness in zero? Why have we created such unfathomable duality? The answer may be that it arises from the world of object relations, where it is absolutely necessary. Mother or father are either present, or they are not. "Zero" is not an abstraction but a concrete experience associated with their absence. It is a deterministic concept and infants, who depend on their parents for internal homeostasis, are motivated to discover the difference between the state of their parents' absence and the opposite, the state of their return—symbolized by "one." Zeros and ones, the abstract language of computers, may be derived directly from the earliest organizing experiences of object relations.

Another scientific concept whose existence is taken for granted is "real time"—yet it, too, is a manufactured abstraction whose nature is becoming more complex (Covency and Highfield 1990). Because we are highly developed entities, humans are probably innately biologically wired with the capacity to organize time just as we are with language. Jacques Lacan, for example, worked at length to synthesize psychoanalytic theory with linguistics, and in the core of his theory the aim of the primary process drive was to establish linguistic meaning for thought and consciousness (Thetford and Walsh 1985). Therefore, one could reasonably expect that just as life organizes itself in the rhythm of time which is

unidirectional, so we too must we have a special orientation
to it. It is in those timed rhythms that we resonate so often
with life around us.

Yet time is uniquely a human experience. From the beginning of life the sense of time—its duration, and the sequence
of events—is associated with primary objects, and is
affectively colored with pleasure or pain. The availability of
objects in time, together with the behavioral responses of the
infant, are mingled with affects that attach to the experience
of the object. Before time as we know it becomes an abstraction at a distance from the self and is measured by clocks, it
is for many years associated primarily with objects and their
affects. Time becomes especially important because it becomes
a reliable means to cope with the anxiety of separation by
predicting the moment of return. According to Arlow, "the
ability to correctly anticipate the immediate future seems to
have a reassuring quality for infants" (Arlow 1989, p. 87).
Thus, time is experienced as *long* when one is in pain or
yearning for the return of a lost object, and is too *short* for
those who are happy and satisfied.

The above examples demonstrate that our ability to formulate abstractions postdates separation-individuation and
is motivated by object relations. Therefore, is not the ability
to cognitively formulate abstract scientific theories based on
physical constructs of space and time that are conditional,
derivative from object relations as were religious beliefs in
our earlier discussion? The human infant, although wired
with the capacity for time sequencing, mathematics, and scientific determinism, may do so in the service of object relations and the security associated with them.

Whether secular or religious, existentialism's claim to a
higher singular truth because of its search for an authentic
"spiritual being" connected with God or the whole of the universe through self-reflection can also be challenged. First of
all, the ability to self-reflect and to experience or observe the
self as an external object is limited. One can do so for only a
relatively short period of time before the mind wanders into

free association. To do so to excess has been considered by some (e. g., Dostoyevsky) a curse or a disease. The emotions associated with the process of self-reflection are often unreproducible even in the same person. As truth, it may be felt deeply, but it is also often transitory.

Secondly, each individual, no matter how self-reflecting or spiritually transcendent, is also caught in a web of observable, rational, interconnected, biological, and social relationships. Systems theory, for example, is the science of those interconnected relationships. It reveals the connections—from the inner makeup of our physiology to the outer world—of the social and physical environment. Our mental and spiritual functioning depend heavily upon our physical state, as well as on the state of our neurophysiology, which is exquisitely sensitive. Consciousness can be disturbed by alterations in homeostasis caused by fever or drugs, or even thrown into disequilibrium and chaotic states that occur in organized dynamic systems (Boldrini 1998, Coveney and Highfield 1990). What we think, feel, and believe is often the combined effect of molecules that wash through our brain, mindlessly. Although we each search for personal meaning we coexist with the rest of life—not necessarily in a spiritual sense but in a factual one—in being self-maintaining, self-organizing, and even self-transcending through evolution. Just as each leaf in its season serves the life of the tree it grows on, so too each individual serves a decidedly social human community. The pursuit of existential truth, while essential, is only one end of the bipolar world that we inhabit, and the experience of which is also colored by the nature of our internal object relations.

PSYCHOANALYSIS AND HERMENEUTICS

Psychoanalysis also laid claim to the possession of truth. Freud repeatedly asserted his view that psychoanalysis was a natural science insofar as it involved the derivation of facts that were observed through the psychoanalytic technique (Bouchard 1995). The facts derived were the reminiscences of the patient held repressed in the unconscious, that give rise to symptoms (Shapiro 1993). Furthermore, Freud adopted a positivist's position that psychoanalysis was universal in its application in art, literature, history, social psychology, and transcultural values. And, to a significant extent, psychoanalysis has had a major impact on western culture in this century. It certainly revolutionized the approach to the mentally ill who, before psychoanalysis, were all too often marginalized in the community or made outcasts by society. Most "talking" psychotherapies employed today owe their acceptance and basic organization to psychoanalytic therapy. The insights of psychoanalysis pervade our culture, from parenting to interpersonal relations, to art and literature. The diffusion of psychoanalytic thought continues to expand everywhere into cultures around the world.

But psychoanalysis had to fail as a natural science because it naively attempted to explain in a deterministic, causal fashion phenomena that were too broad and complex in nature. In most cases it could only approximate relations between reminiscences and specific symptoms. More importantly, it failed to significantly impact the course of illness in many patients, leading to longer, costlier, yet failed treatment. Secondly, psychoanalysis, as the reigning science of mind, was aggressively challenged by the more narrowly conceived neuroscience of the brain with the development of pharmaceutical agents capable of relieving previously unremitting symptoms. Neuroscience has been so successful that the debate today concerning many disorders and with many patients is: "Whether is it mind or brain?" Unfortunately, as a result, too often nowadays we have treatments that are either foolishly mindless or others that are simply brainless. Psychoanalysis's claim to the truth on the basis of science, therefore, was disputed. Thirdly, after Freud, and with the spread of psychoanalysis to many cultures, with their culture-specific languages, values, and schools of practice, the facts derived within psychoanalysis differed with the biases inherent in that culture's set of normative experiences. How could psy-

choanalysis claim to have one language from which all de-
rivative facts could be obtained when it was translated into
so many languages with culture-specific derivatives?

Psychoanalysis has recently undergone a serious transformation from a theoretical preoccupation with the nuances of
metapsychology to hermeneutics, arguments of which spill
across the psychoanalytic literature. Gill is quoted as stating "that his most important theoretical change was the abandonment of metapsychology for hermeneutics" (Chessick 1993,
p. 262).

Hermeneutics is derived from Hermes, the mythological
messenger for the gods. His role was to deliver messages from
the gods to mortals. In order to do so he had to interpret and
understand the message for himself first, and then deliver it
to whom it was intended (Steiner 1995). Hermeneutics refers
to a trend in European philosophy that questions to what
extent an individual's purposes and intentions affect the experience he has and the shape of the reality he apprehends
(Howard 1982). It exists in contrast to natural science where
facts are dispassionately observed. Gadamer, in *Truth and
Method* (1975), persuasively argues that there can never be
one absolute method (science for example) of ascertaining
truth; any method exclusive from all others would necessarily subvert the discovery of truth (Gadamer 1982). With regard to psychotherapy, hermeneutics refers to the nature and
process of deriving understanding in psychotherapy that
arises in a context-dependent relationship and which is therefore true in its own right (Chessick 1995).

Not all psychoanalysts are impressed with the clarity of
the hermeneutic argument and some are concerned about a
potential loss of validity in the psychoanalytic process
(Shapiro 1993). The bedrock of classical theory is that symptoms are the result of reminiscences which are uncovered in
analysis. Do we now state that symptoms are instead the
result of narrative? It is logical enough to state that if experiences of the past affect the present, then appropriate interpretation of the past can ameliorate symptoms in the present.

If, however, a hermeneutic narrative in the present can re-shape the experience of the past, how does it relieve symptoms? The answer may be that it cannot, if one assumes that symptoms in the present are directly causally connected to a specific experience in the past. But if one postulates that an experience in the past affects the arrangement of object relations, then that pathological arrangement of its own nature may maintain symptoms independently of the causative event(s), even if it has been consciously revealed to the patient. This is why "working through" has always been the lion's share of the work in analysis.

Psychoanalysis today recognizes the inherent validity of hermeneutics, especially its conformity with the experience in clinical practice. Psychoanalysis involves context-dependent, dyadic derivation of understanding and meaning between two human beings. It is not entirely an interpretation of a subjective narrative experience because it involves the realism of observation, inquiry, and the uncovering of facts previously held in the unconscious. But it does not cling to the naive realism of an uninvolved observer without influence on the subject. It is at the midpoint between science and history. Psychoanalysis involves a circular dialectic of transference and countertransference, and the effect of those processes on the dynamic narrative; and it occurs temporally, with the revelation of new facts and the shaping of new understanding through repetition. Hermeneutics recognizes the validity of the investigative process within the patient that is continuously reshaping experience, self-symbolizing, and self-transcendent.

Freud's early enthusiasm for the rationalist scientific underpinnings of psychoanalysis and for the universality of its application must also be seen in the appropriate context; Freud was a highly trained physician under the influence of nineteenth-century positivist scientificism together with his considerable personal investment in the humanism derived from the European Enlightenment (Bouchard 1995). Furthermore, even Freud himself, by his discovery of transference and later by his recognition that the analyst and analysand are joined together to reconstruct memories by assembling remembered remains, demonstrated a clear inclination to hermeneutic understandings and derivations (Freud 1937).

SUMMARY

Truth is a complex amalgam of verifiable objective realism of science on one hand and deep subjective, existential experience of personal discovery on the other. There can never be a single unified truth, because we are forever caught in the unresolvable paradox of separation and fusion, which is a reflection of our internal self–object relations. Object relations theory therefore insists that there can be no grand truth in nature and that the search for one is doomed—especially grand theories of union of the psychological mind and the biological brain. All truths are dualistic in nature and are derived from the dyadic nature of object relations. As a theory, object relations explains the persistence of all the philosophical dualities of subject–object existence and causation as well as the drive to union and oneness. Language and notions of space and time—the symbolic media for our intellect and the comprehension of our common experience—are also created and affectively colored by the interplay of internalized object relations. Our explanations of the world, our understanding of our place in it, and our wish to transcend it, no matter how sophisticated they may be, will always be rooted in and simultaneously bounded by the dualities of object relations and the symbolic language and mathematics that flows from them. Truth then is a projection of our internal object relations, fused and separated. We may then believe in God as a means to explain the nature of the universe that we both inhabit and consciously experience, or we may use God to relate with and join to, and in whom we find consolation and peace at times of loss. That object relations may be projected onto an externalized figure who is omnipotent (being both explanatory of the "how" of the universe and the "why" of our personal role in it), while simultaneously being mirroring and self-reflecting, is a choice as authentic in perceiving existence as any another.

Objective and subjective truths occasionally join within analysis, as do states of observation and participation. More frequently, however, one encounters a free-flowing shifting from one mode of participation to another and from one set of truths to another. Psychoanalytic truth as conceived in hermeneutics synthesizes a larger truth than either mode alone. Psychoanalysis should enable the patient to see that we live in a world that is simultaneously deterministic and one in which we are free to choose and be what we may. We must recognize that in psychoanalysis truth does not come easily and that our interpretations are always "inexact." Meaningful truths are frequently surrounded with casual facts and distorted beliefs, and we must have the wisdom to distinguish one from the other. To do this the analyst must recognize that where truth is concerned there are few truths greater than mere kindness.

Finally, it is important to note that the element that gives truth its deep affective feel and powerful appeal is the faith that is attached to it. The greater the faith the greater the sense of the truth. Similarly, profound truths elicit convictions of deep faith. We have previously discussed the role of object relations in the formation of faith. The ability to accept truth depends on the temporal ability to make a leap of faith and to internalize a new configuration of object relations. Even an objective truth carefully crafted will commonly fall on deaf ears. Sometimes the patient is just not ready to place faith in the truth. More than Hermes the messenger god who merely delivers the truth, the psychoanalyst must help prepare the patient to hear the truth, and to do so he or she must encourage the leap of faith, using perhaps the greatest bipolar truth of all: love.

7
Conclusion

He that has and a little tiny wit,—
With hey, ho, the wind and the rain,—
Must make content with his fortunes fit,
For the rain it raineth every day.
                —Shakespeare, *King Lear*, III, ii

The seeking after universal truths is one of the grandest and noblest of human aspirations. Truth, however, is elusive and not easily captured, even by the most learned; many who have claimed to possess it suffer from one of mankind's most common and simple faults: vanity. Thus all of us who try must accommodate ourselves to the misfortune and frustration of our imperfect understanding. This book in many ways is an old story that reaches the same conclusions that so many others, much wiser, have reached across the ages. There is no greater wisdom than kindness and no greater kindness than love. For those with a universalist theistic orientation, that just means that God is immanent and his nature is love.

In the past, analysts believed that they enabled healing through the revelation of reminiscences that were causative agents in the development of the patient's neurotic symptoms. In revealing those singular past experiences analysts felt that they were seeking truth. Truth, as we have shown, is far more complicated than a single past causal experience. The real dyadic relationship with the therapist is perhaps ultimately

more meaningful and perhaps has greater impact for the
eventual outcome of the treatment.

Psychoanalysts have too often taken for granted the patient's expectation of faith in the truthfulness of the analytic
method, and in the past, any challenges to this expectation
were interpreted as resistance. Have we sufficiently considered what this faith is that we have so readily expected from
our patients while they may wander for so long in a desert of
despair? Do we ourselves have faith sufficient to transcend the
pain and suffering that may someday be our own lot to carry?

It is not enough for the analyst to have knowledge or experience. One must also have faith—first in the patient and
then in oneself and one's skills—not only to traverse the gaps
in our understanding but also to forgive our defects and remain secure in our ability to endure the uncertainty of our
treatment. Without faith we may cling too narrowly to rigid
forms of treatment and miss the opportunity to bring about
the powerful potential effect of healing. Given faith's centrality and its powerful influence in human behavior—in equal
standing with scientific rationality—is it not time to develop
an understanding of faith within the larger framework of
scientific medicine and psychiatry?

Object relations theory as an epistemological metaphor informs us that we are born of another and, therefore, forever
organize our experience and understanding of life in a dyadic
relationship to that other. This relationship affects not only
the nature of our faith but also our body image, both physically and mentally. It also affects our susceptibility to depression and shame in reaction to loss and our existential experience of the world that we each must somehow transcend.
Object relations theory therefore has wide implications for
understanding the ambiguities of the truths and falsehoods
in our lives above and beyond its usefulness and value in the
conduct of psychoanalysis.

Life is filled with loss of all kinds, and as we have noted
before, our patients come to us in suffering. They come, too,
with old hurts buried within them. These hurts, tightly bound

up within the internal object relations, are highly organized and, like most diseases, well-defended. As a result of the therapeutic process the patient is able to play out and safely expose the structure of these object relations. In so doing patients make a great leap of faith in revealing the sense of shame and feelings of hurt from the past. They can do so only in a therapeutic environment that is holding, nurturing, and loving.

Being kind, however, does not mean "making nice" but otherwise avoiding uncomfortable truths. We all have immensely destructive narcissistic tendencies, as easily demonstrated by observation of young children at play, who often take just as great pleasure in destroying objects as they do in building them up. Similarly, beyond the hurt and shame of painful experiences suffered from the past, patients often harbor intense hatred and wishes for revenge. Sometimes it is only with forgiveness and the recognition of one's own hurt, which has been bound together with one's own self-righteous hatred and desire for revenge, that one can finally hope to give up the past and create in the present a "good-enough" self, a truthful self in which one can have faith and pride. Ultimately, cure means accepting that one has been loved enough in life even if that love was received relatively late, and perhaps only in analysis. By so doing, one can at last give up one's deep-seated fear and pathological hatred and forgive the world for not having been loved and adored as once upon a time we may have wished for.

References

Angier, N. (1997). Survey of scientists finds a stability of faith in God. *New York Times*, April 3.

Anthony, E. J. (1981). Shame, guilt, and the feminine self in psychoanalysis. In *Object and Self,* ed. S. Tuttman, C. Kaye, and M. Zimmerman, pp. 191–234. New York: International Universities Press.

Antonoff, S. R., and Spilka, B. (1984). Patterning of facial expressions among terminal cancer patients. *Omega* 15:101–108.

Arlow, J. A. (1989). Time as emotion. In *Time and Mind: The Study of Time*, vol. 4, ed. J. T. Fraser, pp. 85–96. Madison, CT: International Universities Press.

Aron, L. (1990). Free association and changing models of mind. *Journal of the American Academy of Psychoanalysis* 18(3):439–459.

Balint, M. (1968). *The Basic Fault: Therapeutic Aspects of Regression*. New York: Brunner/Mazel.

Baudry, F. D., and Wiener, A. (1975). The surgical patient. In *Psychological Care of the Medically Ill*, ed. J. J. Strain and S. Grossman, pp. 123–137. New York: Appleton-Century-Crofts.

Belfer, M. L., Harrison, A. M., Pillemer, F. C., and Murroy, J. E. (1982). Appearance and the influence of reconstructive surgery on body image. *Clinics in Plastic Surgery* 9:307–315.

Boldrini, M., Placidi, G. P. A., and Marazziti, D. (1998). Applications of chaos theories to psychiatry: a review and future perspectives. *CNS Spectrums* 3(1):22–29.

Bouchard, M.-A. (1995). The specificity of hermeneutics in psychoanalysis: leaps on the path from construction to recollection. *International Journal of Psycho-Analysis* 76:533–546.

Bowlby, J. (1960). Grief and mourning in infancy and early childhood. In *Psychoanalytic Study of the Child* 29:107–157. New Haven, CT: Yale University Press.

—— (1961). Process of mourning. *International Journal of Psychoanalysis* 42(4):317–340.

Brenner, C. (1982). *The Mind in Conflict*. New York: International Universities Press.

Breuer, J., and Freud, S. (1893). Studies on hysteria. *Standard Edition* 2:1–18.

Browne, M. W. (1997). Physicists confirm power of nothing, measuring force of universal flux. *New York Times*, January 21, sec. C, p. 1.

Buber, M. (1951). *Two Types of Faith*. New York: Macmillan.

—— (1966). *The Way of Man: According to the Teaching of Hasidism*. Secaucus, NJ: Citadel.

Chessick, R. D. (1977). *Intensive Psychotherapy of the Borderline Patient*. Northvale, NJ: Jason Aronson.

—— (1982). Intensive psychotherapy of a borderline patient. *Archives of General Psychiatry* 39:413–419.

—— (1993). What constitutes our understanding of a patient. *Journal of the American Academy of Psychoanalysis* 21:253–272.

—— (1995). Nothingness, meaninglessness, chaos, and the "black hole" revisited. *Journal of the American Academy of Psychoanalysis* 23(4):581–601.

Clinical Psychiatric News (1996). The role of religion in coping. January, p. 10.

Coen, S. J. (1992). *The Misuse of Persons: Analyzing Pathological Dependency*. Hillsdale, NJ: Analytic Press.

—— (1995). Love between patient and analyst. *Journal of the American Psychoanalytic Association* 43(4):1107 1135.

Coleman, D. (1991). Therapists see religion as aid, not illusion. *New York Times*, September 10.

Coveney, P., and Highfield, R. (1990). *The Arrow of Time*. New York: Fawcett Columbine.

Csordas, T. J. (1990). The psychotherapy analogy and charismatic healing. *Psychotherapy* 27(1):79–90.

Danielian, J., and Lister, E. (1988). The negative therapeutic reaction: the uses of negation. *Journal of the American Academy of Psychoanalysis* 16(4):431–450.

Darwin, C. (1859). *The Origin of Species.* New York: Prometheus.

Durant, W. (1961). *The Story of Philosophy.* New York: Simon & Schuster.

Edgecombe, R. M. (1984). Models of communication: the differentiation of somatic and verbal expression. *Psychoanalytic Study of the Child* 39:137–154. New Haven, CT: Yale University Press.

Eigen, M. (1981). The area of faith in Winnicott, Lacan and Bion. *International Journal of Psycho-Analysis* 62:413–433.

——— (1985). Toward Bion's starting point: between catastrophe and faith. *International Journal of Psycho-Analysis* 66:321–330.

Engel, G. I. (1961). Is grief a disease? *Psychosomatic Medicine* 23(1):18–22.

Erikson, E. (1950). *Childhood and Society.* New York: Norton.

Fairbairn, W. R. D. (1941). A revised psychopathology of the psychoses and psychoneuroses. In *Psychoanalytic Studies of the Personality*, pp. 28–58. London: Routledge & Kegan Paul, 1952.

——— (1952). *Object Relations Theory of the Personality.* New York: Basic Books.

Fenichel, O. (1945). *The Psychoanalytic Theory of Neurosis.* New York: Norton.

——— (1953). *Collected Papers of Otto Fenichel.* New York: Norton.

Frankl, V. (1963). *Man's Search for Meaning.* New York: Simon & Schuster.

Freud, A. (1946). The ego and the mechanisms of defense, rev. ed. In *The Writings of Anna Freud*, vol. 2. New York: International Universities Press.

Freud, S. (1915a). The unconscious. *Standard Edition* 14:159–204.

——— (1915b). Instincts and their vicissitudes. *Standard Edition* 14:109–140.

——— (1917). Mourning and melancholia. *Standard Edition* 14:237–258.

——— (1923). The ego and the id. *Standard Edition* 19:1–59.

——— (1925). An autobiographical study. *Standard Edition* 20:1–70.

——— (1927). The future of an illusion. *Standard Edition* 22:1–56.

——— (1937). Construction in psychoanalysis. *Standard Edition* 23:255–270.

Fromm, E. (1950). *Psychoanalysis and Religion.* New Haven, CT: Yale University Press.

Gabbard, G. O. (1995). Countertransference: the emerging common ground. *International Journal of Psycho-Analysis* 76:475–485.

Gadamer, H. (1975). *Truth and Method.* New York: Crossroads.

Gates of Prayer: The New Union Prayerbook (1975). New York: Central Conference of American Rabbis.

Gay, P. (1988). *Freud: A Life for Our Time.* New York: Norton.

Gill, M. (1982). *Analysis of Transference,* vol. 1: *Theory and Technique.* New York: International Universities Press.

Glover, E. (1949). *Psychoanalysis: A Handbook for Medical Practitioners and Students of Comparative Psychology,* 2nd ed. New York: Staples.

Glucksman, M. L. (1993). Insight, empathy, and internalization: elements of clinical change. *Journal of the American Academy of Psychoanalysis* 21(2):163–181.

Goin, J. M., and Goin, M. K. (1981). *Changing the Body: Psychological Effects of Plastic Surgery.* Baltimore, MD: Williams & Wilkins.

Goldstein, W. N. (1991). Clarification of projective identification. *American Journal of Psychiatry* 148(2):153–161.

Gorman, J. (1997). Consciousness studies: from stream to flood. *New York Times,* April 29, pp. C1, 5.

Greenacre, P. (1958). Early physical determinants in the development of the sense of identity. *Journal of the American Psychoanalytic Association* 6:612–627.

Greenberg, J. R., and Mitchell, S. A. (1983). *Object Relations in Psychoanalytic Theory.* Cambridge, MA: Harvard University Press.

Greenson, R. R. (1961). On the silence and sounds of the analytic hour. *Journal of the American Psychoanalytic Association* 9:79–84.

——— (1965). The working alliance and the transference neurosis. *Psychoanalytic Quarterly* 34:155–181.

——— (1971). The real relationship between the patient and the psychoanalyst. In *Explorations in Psychoanalysis.* New York: International Universities Press, 1978.

Groves, J. E. (1978). Taking care of the hateful patient. *New England Journal of Medicine* 298(16):883–887.

Gunderson, J. G. (1996). The borderline patient's intolerance of aloneness: insecure attachments and therapist availability. *American Journal of Psychiatry* 153(6):752–758.

Guntrip, H. (1971). *Psychoanalytic Theory, Therapy and the Self.* New York: Basic Books.

——— (1975). My experiences of analysis with Fairbairn and Winnicott. *International Review of Psycho-Analysis* 2:145–156.

Hagglund, T., and Heikki, P. (1980). The inner space of the body image. *Psychoanalytic Quarterly* 49:256–283.

Hamlyn, D. W. (1987). *A History of Western Philosophy.* London: Pelican.

Hartmann, H. (1964). *Essays on Ego Psychology.* New York: International Universities Press.

Hayman, A. (1965). Verbalization and identity. *International Journal of Psycho-Analysis* 46:445–466.

Hegel, G. W. F. (1816). *Phenomenology of Spirit.* New York: Oxford University Press, 1979.

Heidegger, M. (1927). *Being and Time.* San Francisco: Harper, 1962.

Howard, R. J. (1982). *Three Faces of Hermeneutics.* Berkeley, CA: University of California Press.

Hundert, E. M. (1989). *Philosophy, Psychiatry and Neuroscience.* Oxford, UK: Clarendon.

Jackel, M. (1966). Transference and psychotherapy. *Psychiatric Quarterly* 40:43–58.

Jacobson, E. (1964). *The Self and the Object World.* New York: International Universities Press.

Jaspers, K. (1959). *Truth and Symbol.* New York: Twayne.

Jenkins, C. D. (1996). While there's hope, there's life. *Psychosomatic Medicine* 58:122–124.

Johnson, S. W. (1992). The listening healer in the history of psychological healing. *American Journal of Psychiatry* 149:1623–1632.

Jones, E. (1952). Preface. In Fairbairn, W. R. D., *Psychoanalytic Studies of the Personality.* London: Routledge & Kegan Paul.

——— (1956a). *Sigmund Freud*, vol. 2. London: Hogarth.

——— (1956b). *Sigmund Freud*, vol. 3. London: Hogarth.

Kafka, E. (1971). On the development of mental self, the bodily self, and self consciousness. *Psychoanalytic Study of the Child* 26:217–240. New Haven, CT: Yale University Press.

Kalick, S. M. (1982). Clinician, social scientist and body image: collaboration and future prospects. *Clinics in Plastic Surgery* 9:379–385.

Kant, I. (1781). *Critique of Pure Reason.* New York: Prometheus, 1990.

Katan, A. (1961). Some thoughts about the role of verbalization in early childhood. *Psychoanalytic Study of the Child* 16:184–188. New York: International Universities Press.

Kendler, K. S., Gardner, C. O., and Presscott, C. A. (1997). Religion, psychopathology, and substance abuse: a genetic-epidemiologic study. *American Journal of Psychiatry* 154(3):322–329.

Kernberg, O. (1980). *Internal World and External Reality.* New York: Jason Aronson.

——— (1984). *Object Relations Theory and Clinical Psychoanalysis.* Northvale, NJ: Jason Aronson.

Kierkegaard, S. (1846). *Concluding Unscientific Postscripts to Philosophical Fragments.* Princeton, NJ: Princeton University Press, 1992.

Knight, R. P. (1953). Borderline states. In *Psychoanalytic Psychiatry and Psychology,* ed. R. P. Knight and C. R. Friedman pp. 97–109. New York: International Universities Press, 1954.

Koenig, H. G., et al. (1992). Religious coping and depression among elderly, hospitalized, medically ill men. *American Journal of Psychiatry* 149(12):1693–1700.

Kohut, H. (1977). *The Restoration of the Self.* New York: International Universities Press.

——— (1984). *How Does Analysis Cure?,* ed. A. Goldberg and P. Stepansky. Chicago: University of Chicago Press.

Kolb, I. C. (1959). Disturbances of body image. In *American Handbook of Psychiatry,* vol. 7, ed. S. Arieti, pp. 749–769. New York: Basic Books.

Kroll, S., and Sheehan, W. (1989). Religious beliefs and practices among 52 psychiatric inpatients in Minnesota. *American Journal of Psychiatry* 146:67–72.

Langs, R., ed. (1981). Truth therapy/lie therapy. In *Classics in Psychoanalytic Technique,* pp. 499–516. New York: Jason Aronson.

Levin, S. (1971). The psychoanalysis of shame. *International Journal of Psycho-Analysis* 52:355–362.

Lewis, H. B. (1987). The role of shame in depression over a lifetime. In *The Role of Shame in Symptom Formation,* pp. 29–50. Hillsdale, NJ: Analytic Press.

Mahler, M. S. (1967). On human symbiosis and the vicissitudes of individuation. *Journal of the American Psychoanalytic Association* 15:740–763.

Mahler, M. S., and McDevitt, J. (1982). Thoughts on the emergence of the sense of self with particular emphasis on the body self. *Journal of the American Psychoanalytic Association* 30:827–848.

Mahler, M. S., Pine, F., and Bergman, A. (1975). *The Psychological Birth of the Human Infant.* New York: Basic Books.

Mann, J. (1962). Clinical and theoretical aspects of religious belief. *Journal of the American Psychoanalytic Association* 12:160.

Meng, H., and Freud, E., eds. (1963). *Psychoanalysis and Faith: The Letters of Sigmund Freud and Oskar Pfister.* New York: Basic Books.

Modell, A. H. (1968). *Object Love and Reality.* New York: International Universities Press.

Nadelson, T. (1996). Psychotherapy, revelation, science and deep thinking: Festschrift in honor of John Nemia, M. D. *American Journal of Psychiatry* (Supp.) 153(7):53–56.

New Union Prayer Book (1975). New York: Central Conference of American Rabbis.

Nietzsche, F. (1883). *Thus Spoke Zarathustra.* In *Basic Writings of Nietzsche.* New York: Modern Library, 1992.

——— (1886). *Beyond Good and Evil.* New York: Random House.

——— (1887). *Genealogy of Morals.* In *Basic Writings of Nietzsche.* New York: Modern Library, 1992.

Nino, A. G. (1990). Restoration of the self: a therapeutic paradigm from Augustine's *Confessions. Psychotherapy* 27(1):8–18.

Nordlicht, S. (1979). Facial disfigurement and psychiatry sequelae. *New York State Journal of Medicine,* August, pp. 1382–1384.

Ogden, T. H. (1983). The concept of internal object relations. *International Journal of Psycho-Analysis* 64:227–241.

Orbach, C. E., and Tallent, N. (1965). Modification of perceived body and of body concepts. *Archives of General Psychiatry* 12:126–135.

Parens, H. (1989). Psychic development during the second and third years of life. In *The Course of Life. Volume 2: Early Childhood,* ed. S. I. Greenspan and G. H. Pollock, pp. 279–334. Madison, CT: International Universities Press.

Pertschuk, M. J., and Whitaker, L. A. (1982). Social and psychological effects of craniofacial deformity and surgical reconstruction. *Clinics in Plastic Surgery* 9:279–306.

Peto, A. (1972). Body image and depression. *Journal of the American Psychoanalytic Association* 53:259–263.

Pollock, G. H. (1978). Process and affect: mourning and grief. *International Journal of Psycho-Analysis* 59:255–276.

Reich, W. (1949). *Character Analysis.* New York: Farrar, Straus, and Young.

Renik, O. (1991). The biblical book of Job, advice to clinicians. *Psychoanalytic Quarterly* 60:596–606.

Retzinger, S. M. (1987). Resentment and laughter: video studies of the shame-rage spiral. In *The Role of Shame in Symptom Formation,* ed. H. B. Lewis, pp. 151–182. Hillsdale, NJ: Analytic Press.

Russek, L. G., and Schwartz, G. E. (1997). Perceptions of parental caring predict health status in midlife: a 35-year follow-up of the Harvard Mastery of Stress Study. *Psychosomatic Medicine* 59(2):144–151.

Sartre, J.-P. (1943). *Being and Nothingness.* New York: Pocket Books, 1956.

Schafer, R. (1968). *Aspects of Internalization.* New York: International Universities Press.

Scharff, J. S. (1992). *Projective and Introjective Identification and the Use of the Therapist.* Northvale, NJ: Jason Aronson.

Scharff, J. S., and Scharf, D. E. (1995). *The Primer of Object Relations Therapy.* Northvale, NJ: Jason Aronson.

Schilder, P. (1935). *The Image and Appearance of the Human Body.* New York: International Universities Press, 1950.

Schopenhauer, A. (1844). *The World as Will and Representation.* New York: Dover, 1969.

Shapiro, T. (1993). On reminiscences. *Journal of the American Psychoanalytic Association* 41:395 101.

Sis, A. C., Passik, S., and Holland, J. C. (1992). The role of spiritual and religious beliefs in patients' level of distress and coping with malignant melanoma. In *Proceedings of the Thirty-Ninth Annual Meeting of the Academy of Psychosomatic Medicine,* San Diego, CA, October 29–November 1, p. 24.

Slakter, E. (1987). *Countertransference: A Comprehensive View of Those Reactions of the Therapist to the Patient that May Help or Hinder Treatment.* Northvale, NJ: Jason Aronson.

Solomon, M. F. (1997). On love and lust in the contertransference. *Journal of the American Academy of Psychoanalysis* 25(1):71–90.

Spinoza, B. (1677). *Ethics,* ed. A. Boyle. New York: Everyman's Publisher, 1993.

Steiner, R. (1995). Hermeneutics or hermes-mess. *International Journal of Psycho-Analysis* 76:435–445.

Stern, C., ed. (1977). *Gates of the House: The New Union Home Prayerbook.* New York: Central Conference of American Rabbis.

Stoudemire, A. (1991). Somatothymia, parts 1 and 2. *Psychosomatics* 32:365–381.

Sutherland, J. D. (1963). Object relations theory and the conceptual model of psychoanalysis. *British Journal of Psychology* 36:109–124.

Tarachow, S. (1963). *An Introduction to Psychotherapy.* New York: International Universities Press.

Taylor, G. J. (1987). *Psychosomatic Medicine and Contemporary Psychoanalysis.* Madison, CT: International Universities Press.

——— (1992). Psychoanalysis and psychosomatics: a new synthesis. *Journal of the American Academy of Psychoanalysis* 20:251–275.

Thetford, W. N., and Walsh, R. (1985). Personality and psychopathology: schools derived from psychology and philosophy. In *Comprehensive Textbook of Psychiatry,* vol. 4, ed. H. I. Kaplan and B. J. Sadock, pp. 459–481. Baltimore, MD: Williams & Wilkins.

Tillich, P. (1957). *Dynamics of Faith.* New York: Harper & Row.

——— (1958). The lost dimension in religion. *Saturday Evening Post* 230(50):29, 76, 78–79.

Tucker, M. E. (1989). Religious beliefs of patients often ignored. *Clinical Psychiatry News* 10:1.

Tuttman, S. (1987). Exploring the analyst's treatment stance in current psychoanalytic practice. *Journal of the American Academy of Psychoanalysis* 15(1):29–37.

Vaillant, G. E. (1985). Loss as a metaphor for attachment. *American Journal of Psychoanalysis* 45(1):59–67.

Wallach, H. F. (1994). Discussion of Lansky: shame—contemporary psychoanalytic perspectives, and Travin and Bluestone: Can the impossible profession help the impossible patient? *Journal of the American Academy of Psychoanalysis* 22(3):443–448.

Wallerstein, R. (1988). One psychoanalysis or many. *International Journal of Psycho-Analysis* 36:3–30.

Winnicott, D. W. (1955). The depressive position in normal emotional development. *British Journal of Medical Psychology* 28:89–100.

——— (1965). *The Maturational Processes and the Facilitating Environment.* New York: International Universities Press.

Wittgenstein, L. (1922). *Tractatus Logico-Philosophicus.* London: Routledge & Kegan Paul, 1995.

Index

ABOUT THE AUTHOR

Harold E. Bronheim, M.D., is Associate Clinical Professor of Psychiatry and Medicine at the Mt. Sinai School of Medicine, and is in private practice in New York City. He is a member of the American Academy of Psychoanalysis and has lectured widely on the role of faith in psychotherapy. Dr. Bronheim is also the chair of the Ad Hoc Task Force for the Academy of Psychosomatic Medicine writing the *Practice Guideline on Psychiatric Consultation in the General Medical Setting.*